Medical Writing

A Guide for Medicos, Educators and Researchers

Medical Writing

A Guide for Medicos, Educators and Researchers

Editor

Putul Mahanta MD FIAMLE FICFMT
Associate Professor
Department of Forensic Medicine and Toxicology
Tezpur Medical College
Tezpur, Assam, India

Forewords

Umesh Chandra Sarma MD (BHU)
Nirmal Chandra Bhattacharyya MS MCh

JAYPEE

JAYPEE BROTHERS MEDICAL PUBLISHERS
The Health Sciences Publisher
New Delhi | London

JAYPEE **Jaypee Brothers Medical Publishers (P) Ltd**

Headquarters
EMCA House
23/23-B, Ansari Road, Daryaganj
New Delhi - 110 002, India
Landline: +91-11-23272143, +91-11-23272703
+91-11-23282021, +91-11-23245672
E-mail: jaypee@jaypeebrothers.com

Corporate Office
4838/24, Ansari Road, Daryaganj
New Delhi - 110 002, India
Phone: +91-11-43574357
Fax: +91-11-43574314
E-mail: jaypee@jaypeebrothers.com

Overseas Office
J.P. Medical Ltd
83 Victoria Street, London
SW1H 0HW (UK)
Phone: +44 20 3170 8910
E-mail: info@jpmedpub.com

EU GPSR Authorised Representative
Logos Europe, 9 rue Nicolas Poussin
17000, La Rochelle, France
Phone: +33 (0) 6 67 93 73 78
E-mail: contact@logoseurope.eu

Website: www.jaypeebrothers.com
Website: www.jaypeedigital.com

Inquiries for bulk sales may be solicited at: jaypee@jaypeebrothers.com

Medical Writing: A Guide for Medicos, Educators and Researchers

First Edition: 2018, *Reprint:* **2026**

ISBN: 978-93-5270-181-0

Printed at: Samrat Offset Pvt. Ltd.

Dedicated to

All the members of the "International Journal of Health Research and Medico Legal Practice".

Esteemed Teachers, Guides and Mentors.

Well-wishers and Readers.

Editorial Board Members

Contributors

Purnima Barua MD
Associate Professor
Department of Microbiology
Jorhat Medical College
Additional Medical Superintendent and
Coordinator of Medical Education Unit at
Jorhat Medical College
Jorhat, Assam, India

Nirmal Chandra Bhattacharyya MS MCh
Former Professor of Pediatric Surgery and
Principal-cum-Chief Superintendent
Tezpur Medical College and Hospital
Tezpur, Assam, India

Roonmoni Deka MS PhD
Professor and Head
Department of Anatomy
Tezpur Medical College
Tezpur, Assam, India

Rup Sekhar Deka MBBS LLB MD PhD
Associate Professor
Department of Anatomy
Gauhati Medical College
Guwahati, Assam, India

Junu Devi MD PhD
Associate Professor
Department of Pathology
Assam Medical College
Dibrugarh, Assam, India

Putul Mahanta MD FIAMLE FICFMT
Associate Professor
Department of Forensic Medicine
and Toxicology
Tezpur Medical College
Tezpur, Assam, India

AJ Patowary MD FNFCFM
Professor and Head
Department of Forensic Medicine
and Toxicology
North Eastern Indira Gandhi Regional
Institute of Health and Medical Sciences
Shillong, Meghalaya, India

Hiranya Saikia MSc M Phil PhD
Senior Lecturer in Biostatistics
Assam Medical College
Dibrugarh, Assam, India

Anku Moni Saikia MD
Professor
Department of Community Medicine
Assam Medical College
Dibrugarh, Assam, India

Dipak Kumar Sarma MS FAIS FIAGES FMAS
Professor
Department of Surgery
Assam Medical College and Hospital
Dibrugarh, Assam, India

Mukesh Yadav MD MBA (HCA) LLB PGDHOQM PGDHR FICFMT FAHA
Principal and Professor
Department of Forensic Medicine and Toxicology
NC Medical College
Panipat, Haryana, India

Foreword

The first edition of the book *Medical Writing: A Guide for Medicos, Educators and Researchers* edited by Dr Putul Mahanta, very categorically meet out the objectives of research and publications. Research publication and dissemination of academic knowledge in Medical education are among the most important and an essential requisite of academic scholars, and MCI makes it mandatory for the faculties working in medical colleges as a promotional criteria. However, such experience and skills are rarely taught, transferred and shared in the academic curriculum. This multi-authored book is a sincere attempt to help the faculty members of institutions of health sciences, young research workers, medical and allied life science graduates and also the reviewers. This book will really be useful for the undergraduate and postgraduate students of Medicine, Dentistry, AYUSH, Pharmacy, Nursing, Biotechnology, Cellular and Molecular Biology and other Public Health related subjects. Such kind of multi-authored book is very rare, where more than a dozen of experienced faculties of various medical colleges of national and international repute contributed and have been reviewed by competent reviewers. The book contents will give the basic concepts for research and publications to the readers to improve the skill of medical writing. The book has widely discussed the legal and ethical matter highlighting some of the relevant issues, which will help the readers to avoid research and publication misconduct.

I strongly recommend this book for all the researchers. I hope, the editors will include in the subsequent edition other issues, like how to write a postgraduate and doctoral thesis, project reports, critical review, and letter to editor, etc.

Umesh Chandra Sarma MD (BHU)
MSc in Epidemiology (London University)
PG Training in Epidemiology (London University)
Vice Chancellor
Srimanta Sankaradeva
University of Health Sciences
Guwahati, Assam, India

Foreword

The art of writing a scientific document in medical and related area, whether it is a report of scientific research, journal manuscript, drug related promotional literature, or news article, requires knowledge and understanding of the medical concept and terminology, technical guidelines for writing specific documents, basic knowledge of statistics, ethical and legal issues concerning research publications, expertize in searching literature and above all a good writing skill. Medical Writing has become a specialty on its own, although the conventional medical curriculum does not include it. However, any research worker in the medical, pharmaceutical, nursing, dental, public health, biological and life science fields must have good knowledge about medical writing. The knowledge of medical writing is also essential for the postgraduate students and PhD scholars of medical and allied sciences for writing thesis and research articles for publication. The compulsory requirement of a minimum number of publications as a benchmark for promotion of faculty members, as stipulated by the Medical Council of India has made it mandatory for all medical teachers to learn how to write articles for publication in an indexed medical journal.

The present endeavor to publish a handbook on Medical Writing is aimed at reaching out to the young research workers, postgraduate students, PhD scholars and also medical educators, to assist them in acquiring knowledge and skill in writing articles for publication, preparing thesis and also make them understand the ethical and legal issues on the subject.

The International Journal of Health Research and Medico Legal Practice (IJHRMLP) Academic is a vibrant group of like-minded young and energetic faculty members drawn from various Medical Colleges of Assam, which in a short span of time has arranged a number of CME programs on a wide range of health related contemporary issues, workshops on research methodology, and other academic activities in the field of Medical education. It also publishes the "International Journal of Health Research and Medico Legal Practice", a multi-disciplinary peer-reviewed indexed medical journal. The IJHRMLP Academic, in its continuing effort to upgrade the academic environment in the field of Medical Education in the State has taken up the task of publishing the first edition of a Handbook on Medical Writing. The subsequent editions are planned to include topics, like thesis writing, preparation of research project and other related subjects.

I hope that the first edition of the Handbook on Medical Writing will be a great help to the postgraduate students, research workers and medical teachers.

Nirmal Chandra Bhattacharyya MS MCh
Former Professor of Pediatric Surgery and
Principal-cum-Chief Superintendent
Tezpur Medical College and Hospital
Tezpur, Assam, India

Preface

While I was pursuing my postgraduation, I felt the need of a good guidebook on medical writing with illustrations, tables, flowcharts and the valid references for faster and better comprehension. The problem continued when I joined as faculty in a medical college.

As a medical college faculty, and as an editor of a textbook and journal, I have seen many of the foreign medical writings on our profession that have been written elaborately, explained with beautiful illustrations and flushed with plenty of high-resolution photographs. They also cite the references in a scientific way, which are essential for the readers to understand the source of the text. And, thus, the idea of editing a guidebook shaped in my mind.

This guidebook is targeted mainly for the students of Medicine, Dentistry, Ayurveda, Pharmacy, Nursing, Biotechnology, Cellular and Molecular Biology and other Public Health-related subjects, both undergraduate and postgraduate. I hope it would be useful not only for all those mentioned, but also for research scholars working in different fields.

The book contains 12 chapters that have eleven experienced contributors of national and international repute, competent editors, reviewers and proofreaders.

A good number of new topics like "Ethical and Legal Issues in Research and Publication" and ideas like "Road Map of Submitting Manuscript for Best Acceptance", have increased the depth and width of the book. All the text illustrations are updated with recent amendments on research and publication.

Emphasis has been given to include some unfamiliar terms, like research misconduct, ghost authorship, and related ethical and legal issues.

I sincerely hope this book will serve the intent and purpose and help the readers learn the basics of medical writing. All the positive critiques will be the strength for further improvement of this book.

Putul Mahanta MD FIAMLE FICFMT

Acknowledgments

Editing any book is an enormous job. It would not have been possible to edit this book without the help and support of the distinguished people around me.

As many as 11 experts have contributed chapter materials including some illustrations. I sincerely hope that these contributions will definitely benefit the readers. To name few legends: Prof Nirmal Chandra Bhattacharyya, Prof Roonmoni Deka, Prof Anku Moni Saikia, Prof AJ Patowary, Prof Mukesh Yadav, Dr Dipak Kumar Sarma, Dr Junu Devi, Dr Purnima Barua, Dr Rup Sekhar Deka and Dr Hiranya Saikia were my constant source of inspiration.

Prof Umesh Chandra Sarma, Vice Chancellor and Prof BK Bezbaruah, Registrar, Srimanta Sankaradeva University of Health Sciences, Guwahati, Assam deserve deepest gratitude for their continuous support and advice.

Detailed chapter reviews were accredited to help me established the necessary changes required for the book and I am extremely grateful to Dr Kahua Das Thakuria for reviewing and proofreading all the chapters in time.

I had to implore, borrow and take some of the text that appear in this book from my colleagues and from different sources. I am grateful to them for their support. They are acknowledged on the respective pages. My colleague Prof Gunajit Das needs special mention for his suggestions on different issues.

All the editorial board members, reviewers and advisors both national and international of "International Journal of Health Research and Medico Legal Practice (IJHRMLP)" deserve special thanks for their persistent support and encouragement towards our academic activities. I am also thankful to all the supporting staff of our Journal, i.e., IJHRMLP.

I am especially grateful to Jaypee Brothers Medical Publishers, for their expertise in the shaping, collation and illustration of this book.

Since the preparation of this book my wife, Manmi Das Mahanta has encouraged me consistently and typed some of the texts throughout the period. Any large endeavor of this type can't be complete without the support of any family and my family is of no exception. My wife, son Jacinth and daughter Adriana deserve special mention. I thank them for their tolerance for my absences, physically and emotionally during this period.

Putul Mahanta MD FIAMLE FICFMT

Contents

CHAPTER

1

Authorship

Putul Mahanta

AUTHORSHIP

Academic authorship of journal articles, books or project report is a means through which author/s share the results of their scholarly work, establish importance for their discoveries, and build their reputation among their peers.

In academic publishing, authorship of a work is claimed by those making intellectual contributions to the completion of the research described in the work. In many disciplines, however, collaboration is the norm and issues of authorship can be controversial. In these contexts, authorship can encompass activities other than writing the article; a researcher who comes up with an experimental design and analyzes the data may be considered an author, even if she or he had a little role in composing the text describing the results. According to some standards, even writing the entire article would not constitute authorship unless the writer was involved in at least one or other phase of the project.[1,2]

Authorship confers credit and has important academic, social, and financial implications. Authorship also implies responsibility and accountability for published work.

WHO IS AN AUTHOR?

The International Committee of Medical Journal Editors (ICMJE) recommended the following four criteria for the authorship:[2,3]

1. Author must substantially contribute to the conception, designing of the work, acquisition, analysis, or interpretation of data related to the study.
2. Not only drafting of the work, but also revising it judgmentally for drawing scholarly content.
3. Have to approve the final version of the paper for publication
4. Agreement to the accountability of all related aspects of the study with regards to integrity and accuracy of the topic investigated thereof and resolved.

STANDARDS OF AUTHORSHIP

The standard of authorship of a scholarly writing existed to those scholars who have contributed genuinely and in a substantial way to draw its scholarly content. All authors should be responsible for honestly assessing their parts in the research study. The coauthors ensure that coauthorship is credited to them according to the standard practices of scholarly research and publications for which they will be listed as an author.

REQUIREMENT OF ATTRIBUTION[4]

Each author should have participated sufficiently in the work to take public responsibility for its integrity and accountability of the content. All authors should attribute as per the following criteria:

1. Planning and contribution to some modules (conception, design, conduct, analysis, or interpretation of data) of the study which led to the paper or interpreting at least a portion of the results of the study.
2. Writing a draft of the paper or revising it critically for scholarly content; and
3. Final approval of the paper to be published. All authors should review and approve the manuscript before it is submitted to a journal for publication, at least as it pertains to their roles in the study project.

However, some diversity existed across the academic disciplines regarding the acceptability of standards for indispensable contributions that would lead to attribution of authorship.

"Gaining of funding", or general supervision of the researchers alone does not constitute authorship. Many medical journals have unrestricted the strict concept of authorship, with the flexible concept of contributor to the study.[5] The number of authors are increasing day by day. Between 1980–2010, the average number of authors in medical papers has increased and perhaps tripled.[6]

ORDER OF AUTHORS IN THE PAPER

Rules for the order of multiple authors in a scientific paper have historically varied.[7] Certain fields list authors in order of their degree of contribution in the research, with the most active contributors listed first; other fields, such as mathematics or engineering (e.g. control theory), sometimes list them alphabetically.[8-10] Historically, biologists tended to place a principal investigator (supervisor or lab head) last in an author list whereas organic chemists might have put him or her first.[11] Research articles in high energy physics, where the author lists can number in tens to hundreds, often list authors alphabetically. In computer science, in general, the principal contributor is the first in the author list. However, the practice of putting the principal investigator last in the author list has increasingly become an accepted standard norm across most areas in science and engineering.

Although listing authors in order of the involvement in the project seems straightforward, it often leads to conflict. A study in the Canadian Medical Association Journal found that more than two-thirds of 919 corresponding authors disagreed with their coauthors regarding contributions of each author.[12]

LISTING OF AUTHOR

There are many ways of listing of authors. One of the important styles is the "Vancouver system" which is commonly used in medical and scientific writings. Followings are the ways of listing the authors as per Vancouver style:

Name/s of Author/s, Editor/s, Compiler/s or the Institution Responsible

- When author numbers are six or less than six, name them all. All the authors must be listed.

- Where author numbers are seven or more, only the first six authors should be listed and should add "et al." (et al. means "and others").
- Coma should be there with a space in between each name with full stop with the last name after their initial(s).

Format of listing the authors: Surname (1 space) initial/s (no spaces or punctuation between initials) (full stop OR if further names comma, 1 space)

Example: Mahanta PK, Patowary AJ, editors.

Example: Mahanta PK, Patowary AJ, Sarma DK, Deka RC, Ahmed AK, Kumar Manoj N, et al.

Example: The Neurology Society of India and Canada.

When no author is given, "Anonymous" or "Anon" is unnecessary. The title of the article or the book should be used.

FIRST AUTHOR AND CORRESPONDING AUTHOR

First author of a research publication is usually the primary investigator who has to carry out the research along with others. He may also be called as presenting author of the paper. The first author is responsible for undertaking the research work practically along with other coauthors. The coauthor may assist him in the research procedures as a research group or some other ways. He is in authority for preparing the manuscript and analyzing the data.

Corresponding author, on the other hand, is the senior author who provides the scholarly effort, helps in designing the proposal and approves the procedures to be followed in the research study. The corresponding author is accountable for the paper correction, proofreading, and entire correspondence during the paper submission to the journal. He also handles the revisions and resubmission procedures of revised manuscripts up to the acceptance of the paper. This is the normal practice usually carried out in most of the cases.

Even the research is carried out in association with some establishments, the first author and corresponding author remains the same, but the number of coauthors increases. This increased number of coauthors depends on the number of helping hands.

Many academicians consider that the first author carries out the greater part of the research––designs, interprets and writes the manuscript. According to them, the corresponding author, in most of the cases, is the principal investigator who has major involvement in the designing of the research. He also supervises the research besides data analysis.[13] The corresponding author is the author who is responsible for all contact and correspondence in future in relation to submission of their manuscript with the journal.

CONTRIBUTORS OTHER THAN AUTHOR

The contributors of the manuscript who do not qualify any criteria as mentioned by ICMJE for authorship should not be mentioned as coauthor, etc. All those should be acknowledged duly in the acknowledgement section after the conclusion.

For example:

- Acquisition of funding
- Writing assistance
- Technical editing
- Language editing

- Proofreading
- General supervision of a research group
- General administrative support.

All the above mentioned fields can be acknowledged individually or together as a group under a common heading, viz., clinical investigators, participating investigators, blood bank stuff, etc. Their contribution must be specified in the declaration, i.e. served as scientific advisors, critically reviewed the research proposal, collected and complied data, participated in writing or technical editing of the manuscript, etc.[14]

ISSUE OF AUTHORSHIP AND MEDICAL COUNCIL OF INDIA/DENTAL COUNCIL OF INDIA REGULATIONS[15]

The Medical Council of India's (MCI) initial rules for elevation to the position of associate professor and professor state a compulsory publication of at least two research papers by the applicants.[13] In September 2015, the MCI issued a "clarification" on what constitutes "research publications" for elevation of teaching faculty of medical colleges/institutions in India (Box 1.1).[16]

Ghost Authorship

It is basically the reverse of honorary authorship, involving one who does significant contribution to a research and manuscript preparation, but do not accept any acknowledgement of his contribution. In the most common circumstances, professional medical writer or an industry researcher make draft research paper on behalf of a pharmaceutical company, but he is not credited for this work.

Box 1.1: Guidelines for counting research publications for promotion of teaching faculty of medical colleges/institutions in India as laid down in an order by MCI in September 2015

a. *Index agencies:* Scopus, PubMed, Medline, Embase/Excerpta Medica, Index Medicus and Index Copernicus
b. *Types of articles to be considered:* Original research articles and original research papers
c. *Criteria for national/international journal:* Published by a national/international—specialty journal/journal of a national/international society provided it is included in one of the indexes mentioned above
d. *Authorship:* First author and second author
e. *E-journals:* E-journals not included.

The above would also be applicable for "accepted for publication" papers/articles.

These ghostwriters may conceal well known industry backing for research, improving the apparent objectivity of a paper while maintaining the company's control over its content. This concealment is often coupled with guest authorship, the practice of adding a reputable academic researcher's name to a manuscript to increase its credibility, despite little to no actual involvement.[17]

"Guest authorship is also known as "honorary authorship", where a person is listed as an author who has not contributed anything to the study[18,19] but become the author. In conclusion, whether or not a ghost author is a secret author, concealing his/her contributions to a manuscript are an unethical practice or research misconduct that violates the current guidelines for authorship and is increasingly targeted by future policies.

REFERENCES

1. Dickson JG, Conner RN, Adair KT. Guidelines for Authorship of Scientific Articles. Wildl Soc Bull 1978;6(4):260-1.
2. ICMJE. Defining the role of authors and contributors. [cited 2017 May 25]; Available from: URL:http://www.icmje.org/recommendations/browse/roles-and-responsibilities/defining-the-role-of-authors-and-contributors.html
3. Majumder K. Editage Insights. Publication Ethics. The final manuscript should be approved by the co-authors before submission. [cited 2017 June 2]; Available from: URL:http://www.editage.com/insights/the-final-manuscript-should-be-approved-by-the-coauthors-before-submission
4. Informs Pubsonline. Marketing Science 2017. [cited 2017 June] Available form: URL:http://pubsonline.informs.org/page/mksc/submission-guidelines
5. Rennie D, Yank V, Emanuel L. When authorship fails: A proposal to make contributors accountable. JAMA 1997;278(7):579-85.
6. Tsao CI, Roberts LW. Authorship in scholarly manuscripts: practical considerations for resident and early career physicians. Acad Psychiatry 2009;33(1):76-9.
7. Kennedy D. On Academic Authorship (RPH 2.8). Stanford University Research Policy Handbook Document 2.8. 1985.
8. Stubbs C. The serious business of listing authors. Nature 1997; 388(6640):320.
9. Rules for submission of abstracts to EPAC96. European Particle Accelerator Conference 1996 (EPAC'96). Barcelona, Spain; 1995.
10. Guidelines for the Preparation of Abstracts. Seventh biennial International Conference on Accelerator and Large Experimental Physics Control Systems (ICALEPCS'99). Trieste, Italy; 1998.
11. Credit where credit's due. Nature 2006;440(7084):591-2.
12. Ilakovac V, Fister K, Marusic M, et al. Reliability of disclosure forms of authors' contributions. CMAJ 2007;176(1):41-6.
13. Difference between corresponding author and first author and what are all their responsibilities? [Cited 2017 May 18]; Available from: URL:https://www.researchgate.net/post/Difference_between_Corresponding_author_and_First_author_and_what_are_all_their_responsibilities

14. Journal of Caring Sciences. Instructions for authors. [cited 2017 June 2]; Available from: URL:http://journals.tbzmed.ac.ir/JCS/ForAuthors
15. Aggarwal R, Gogtay N, Kumar R, et al. Guest Editorial. The revised guidelines of the Medical Council of India for academic promotions: Need for a rethink. Indian J Pharmacol 2016;48(2):111-3.
16. Medical Council of India. (2015). Clarification with regard to research publications in the matter of promotion for teaching faculty in a medical college/institutions. [cited 2015 Dec 8]; Available from: URL:http://www.mciindia.org/circulars/Circular-03.09.2015-TEQ-Promotion-Publication.pdf
17. Rosenberg LE. Physician–scientists—endangered and essential. Science 1999;283:331-2.
18. Wyngaarden JB. The clinical investigator as an endangered species. N Engl J Med 1979;301:1254-9.
19. Panter Michaela. American Journal Experts. Ghost Authorship. [cited 2017 June 1]; Available from: URL:http://www.aje.com/en/arc/ghost-authorship/

CHAPTER

2

'Title' of a Research Paper

Rup Sekhar Deka, Anku Moni Saikia

The first thing that attracts the readers to go through a research article is obviously its "title". The context of the research work is exhibited in the title in a concise manner. Construction of an article's "title" has a significant impact on acceptance and frequency of citation of a research paper.[1] Journal websites, database and search engines use the words from the title to categorize the topic. It is very usual that readers first consider the title to determine whether to go through it or not.[2-4]

There are three main types of title, viz., declarative, descriptive and interrogative. Declarative title exhibits the main findings or conclusion, whereas a descriptive title does not divulge the findings. In the latter, result of the topic remains suspense to the readers and as such, the reader may feel to go through the whole article.

In a declarative title, as the result is declared, so curiosity of reader may be lost to read the full article. Only those results which are unequivocal, definitive and unchallengeable should be declared. Interrogative title states the research hypothesis in a question form.

Some titles may have subtitles which are basically added to provide additional information (Compound titles).[5] For example, let us consider a research title––"Obesity, nonvegetarian diet and the risk of coronary heart disease among adults of the Indian subcontinent: A case-control study". Here, the symbol "colon" has been used to provide some additional information, i.e. the study design. In the field of medicine, the recommended and commonly used title is a descriptive one.[6]

A good "title" not only catches the readers' attention, but also helps in specializing the particular article from other articles on the same topic.[6] However, there are no specified guidelines for construction of a "title". It has been described and understood in various ways by different bodies.

CHARACTERISTICS OF A GOOD TITLE

- The title should be always informative. It should be neither too short nor too long. A short title may fail to reveal the primary objectives of the research. A lengthy title may be tedious enough to distract the readers. However, studies have shown that articles with short titles attract higher viewing and citations.[6,7] There is no consensus on the number of words or characters in a title. It varies from journal to journal. Many leading research journals impose a limit of 10–12 words.[3]
- It should be continuous so as to be useful in indexing. Broken sentences and use of hyphen are not acceptable.
- A title should be comprehensive and self-explanatory. Incorporation of the keywords makes the title sufficiently informative to convey the essence of the article.

- The title is, as a matter of fact, a short "telegraphic summary" of the objectives.[8] Central objectives and key variables should be apparent in the title.[9]
- Place and the type of study design should be mentioned in relevant situations.[8] For example, in the study "Prevalence of elder abuse among community dwelling elderly of Guwahati City, Assam", there is no need to mention the study design in the title. It is implied that this is a cross-sectional study (Prevalence). The *British Medical Journal* recommends titles to include the study design in case of original research.[10] Again, mentioning the place of study in the title may only attract the readers of certain geographic areas.
- Specification of the study population is an important part of the title.[8] It helps the readers to make choice in relation to age groups, ethnicity, etc.
- Redundant phrasing, such as, "A Study of", "An Analysis of" or similar constructions are to be avoided.[5,11] Use of these types of phrases do not influence the impact of the title, rather increases the length of it.
- *Use of unfamiliar* abbreviations, acronyms and jargons is not recommended. However, standard and well-known abbreviations can be used in "title".[5,11]
- Taking care of correct grammar and punctuation is crucial. It is better to avoid excess punctuation, commas and terms in quotes.[12]
- Any numerical value of the parameters should not be mentioned in the title.[5]

To summarize, a good title is simple, short yet informative, specific with regard to purpose/results and adheres to the norms specified above.

THE TITLE WRITING PROCESS[13]

Finally, let us consider an example, "Obesity, nonvegetarian diet and the risk of coronary heart disease among adults of 40–60 years of age of the Indian subcontinent: A case-control study". This title has been framed in different steps, each step answering some specific questions as follows:

1. Identifying the purpose (Relationship among obesity, nonvegetarian diet and coronary heart disease) and the results obtained (Obesity and nonvegetarian diet are risk factors of coronary heart disease).
2. Finding out the study design (Case-control study), the participants (Adults of 40–60 years) and geographical location (Indian subcontinent).
3. Choosing the keywords and key phrases (Case-control study, obesity, nonvegetarian diet, coronary heart disease, 40–60 years of age, India, at risk) and use them in drafting the title.
4. Formulating a working title at the beginning, finally editing it by omission of unessential and repetitive words.

The process of title writing extends from beginning of the concept till the final conclusion. During this period, it may vary on several occasions and the best one has to be adopted at the last. A title should not be finalized in a hurry.

REFERENCES

1. Jacques TS, Sebire NJ. The impact of article titles on citation hits: an analysis of general and specialist medical journals. JRSM Short Rep 2010;1:2.
2. International Committee of Medical Journal Editors. Uniform requirements for manuscripts submitted to biomedical journals: Writing and editing for biomedical publication. [cited 2017 June 3]; Available from: URL:http://www.ICMJE.org
3. Fathalla MF, Fathalla MMF (2004). A Practical Guide for Health Researchers. [cited 2017 June 3]; Available from URL:http://www.emro.who.int/dsaf/dsa237.pdf
4. SAGE Publications. Help Readers Find Your Article. [cited 2017 June 3]; Available from: URL:http://www.uk.sagepub.com/journalgateway/findArticle.htm
5. Bavdekar SB. Formulating the Right Title for a Research Article. J Assoc Physicians India 2016;64:53-6.
6. Jamali HR, Nikzad M. Article title type and its relation with the number of downloads and citations. Scientometrics 2011;88:653-61.
7. Grant MJ. What makes a good title? Health Infor Libr J 2013;30:259-60.
8. Bhalwar R. Textbook of Public Health and Community Medicine. 1st ed. Pune: Department of Community Medicine, Armed Forces Medical College; 2009. p. 197.
9. Goyal RC. Research Methodology for Health Professionals. [cited 2017 June 3]; Available from: URL:https://books.google.co.in/books?isbn=9350251019
10. British Medical Journal. Title page. 2012. [cited 2017 June 3]; Available from: URL:http://www.bmj.com/about-bmj/resources-authors/forms-policies-and-checklists/title-page
11. Sacred Heart University Library. Organizing Academic Research Papers: Choosing a Title. [online]. [cited 2017 June 2017]; Available from: URL:http://library.sacredheart.edu/c.php?g=29803&p=185911
12. Neill US. How to write a scientific masterpiece. J Clin Invest. 2007; 117:3599-602.
13. Bioscience Writers. Writing Strong Titles for Research Manuscripts. [cited 2017 June 3]; Available from: URL:www.biosciencewriters.com/Writing-Strong-Titles-for-Research-Manuscripts.aspx

CHAPTER 3

Abstract and Keywords

Roonmoni Deka

In the preparation of a research paper, research proposal or grant proposal, constructing a concise structured abstract is a crucial part. Essentially, an abstract is a brief synopsis or summary of the most important points that the author makes in the paper. It is a highly condensed version of the paper itself.[1]

Defining an Abstract

The word "abstract" has been derived from a Latin word "abstractum" meaning a condensed form of a longer piece of writing. It is primarily of two types depending on the discipline of the work:[2]

1. *Descriptive*: A descriptive abstract states briefly the type of information found in the work without making any judgments or expressing opinions. It may be a collation of various opinions or works on a particular topic or a mere statement of the contents of the actual paper. It usually does not provide results or conclusions of the research. These are generally very short (50–100 words).

2. *Informative*: Most abstracts are informative. Informative abstracts go further than descriptive abstracts and summarize all the main points, primary results and conclusions of the complete paper. Scientific papers usually use informative abstracts. These provide an essence of the report in about 200–250 words.

Why Do We Actually Write an Abstract?

An abstract is to a written work what a trailer is to a full-length movie. It is a short summary of the complete research. It is the pivot of a paper because manuscripts are screened on the basis of the abstract. It is important to remember that time is of the essence in most editorial processes. If the abstract fails to make a good first impression, in most cases, the paper will be summarily rejected leaving no scope for further consideration regardless of its substantive merit. Further, it is the first thing that the readers will access, whether in a journal or through any type of electronic search engine to get a quick overview of the whole paper. The abstract constitutes the basis of a reader's decision to download or purchase any academic writing online and to read further on in print journals.[3] Similarly, it is the only part of the paper that is published in conference proceedings. Put simply, a well-written abstract piques the readers' interest and makes them want to learn more about the research.

What Makes a Good Abstract?

A good abstract comprises of a single well-written comprehensive paragraph. It includes the essential features of the full paper and is complete in itself. It is written as simply as possible depending on the nature and contents of the paper. It is important that the text flows. It should not be a collection of disjointed sentences.[4,5] It should be written in a manner that is comprehendible by both experts in the specific field as well as general readers with some knowledge of the field.[6] It should not contain any information which is not included in the paper. It should broadly reflect the language of the full paper in a concise yet accessible form. Referencing is neither essential nor advisable in an abstract.[7] In most scientific publications, the abstract is placed at the beginning of the paper. In some cases, depending on the editorial requirements, it may be placed in a separate page.

Formatting an Abstract

The format to be used for the abstract depends on its purpose. If the writing is for a specific publication, specific guidelines of the journal, in which the article is to be published, are to be followed.[8] Abstracts for a conference paper should tell what the study is all about, thereby eliciting the interest of the participants in attending the talk.

The basic components of an abstract are as follows:[9]

1. *Statement of issue/problem*: Why is the selected topic an issue of interest or relevance? What is the specific scientific or academic lacunae that it proposes to bridge? In other words, the backdrop of the study must be delineated in the abstract.
2. *Methodology*: What path has been adopted to obtain the specified targets?
3. *Results/outcomes*: As a consequence of completing the above mentioned procedure, what was learnt?

Table 3.1: Structure of a scientific abstract

Section	*Content of each section*
Introduction	Brief statement of the backdrop of the study.
Aims	The goals sought to be achieved by the academic enquiry.
Methods	The specific methods employed to attain the goals mentioned above.
Results and observations	The final findings of the enquiry.
Conclusion	Concluding remarks and inferences drawn.

4. *Conclusion*: What are the larger implications of the findings, specifically in light of the problem outlined in step 1?

Each of the above sections should be limited to two or three sentences.

The ideal structure of a scientific abstract is summarized in Table 3.1 with each section having specific headings:[10]

The entire abstract should ideally be completed within 200–250 words.

When and How to Write the Abstract?

The abstract should be written only after the paper has been completed in entirety.[11] This is for the reason that a condensed form of the paper cannot be structured unless there is absolute clarity with respect to its findings and conclusions. There are certain dos and don'ts that must be kept in mind while writing abstracts.[12-14]

The Dos

While writing an abstract, the author must appropriately extract key sentences or ideas from the central hypotheses of the paper, objectives sought to be achieved, the methods employed to achieve these objectives and the results obtained by implementing these methods. Finally, the extracted sentences or ideas must be arranged into one logical paragraph ideally in the following sequence: introduction, aims, methods, results and conclusions. The sentences are to be linked to ensure that the information flows well. There should be consistency between the information presented in the abstract and in the paper. A colleague may preferably be asked to review the abstract and check if the purpose, aims, methods, and conclusions of the study are clearly stated and in consonance with the actual contents of the paper. It needs to be checked whether the final abstract meets the requisites of the relevant journal with respect to word limit, chapterization, etc. Finally, the abstract should be revisited and revised with the foregoing steps in mind, to enhance its readability, conciseness and its ability to capture the reader's interest.[15]

The Don'ts

The abstract should not contain new information that is not present in the paper such as undefined abbreviations or group names, a discussion of previous literature, reference or citations, and unnecessary details about the methods used.

Thus, to a reader, a paper is nothing more than what its abstract claims it to be. The abstract determines whether readers find it of interest to read the full paper. There exists, therefore, an ethical obligation on part of the author to make certain that the abstract is an honest representation of the whole paper.

KEYWORDS

Keywords are a tool that leads researchers to academic works of relevance to their interests. Often, researchers may not be cognizant of information published in journals or other publications that they do not regularly browse. Alternatively, the title of an academic work may not always be clearly representative of its content. In such situations, they may resort to a keyword search in order to arrive at a collection of potentially relevant academic information. To illustrate this, we may take assistance from an example––A paper could be titled "Biopsy Techniques for Ocular Tumors" explaining various methods of surgically removing tissues for histopathological examination. However, the title may not directly mention each specific method discussed and the text of the article may include information beyond the title. Thus, to make this paper appear in relevant searches, suitable keywords such as 'eye tumors', 'malignancy', or the names of specific biopsy techniques should be included. Usually, words present in the title should not be included as keywords since they are already considered when a search is carried out. The idea behind employing keywords is to enhance and add on to what is included in the title.

In other words, keywords serve as additional pointers to the paper making it more searchable and ensuring for it adequate numbers of citations.[16]

How should Appropriate Keywords be Picked?

The following must be kept in mind while choosing keywords:[17,18]

- Important words and phrases that are used frequently or repetitively in the writing must be included.
- Other phrases, deemed crucial to the key ideas of the paper, may also be included.
- Common synonyms of terms used must also be listed (e.g. hepatic and liver).
- Common acronyms or abbreviations of relevant terms should be included.

Once the above is done, reference should be made to a common vocabulary or indexing standard followed in the field. A few examples of such standards are:[19]

- GeoRef
- ERIC Thesaurus
- PsycInfo
- ChemWeb
- BIOSIS Search Guide
- MeSH Thesaurus (Medical Subject Headings).

Finally, a search should be run using the selected keywords to verify their appropriateness and to be certain that the said keywords lead to results that resemble the contents of the paper.

To summarize, while writing powerful abstracts and selecting the right keywords may seem difficult, the importance of these two short segments of a paper cannot be overemphasized. As mentioned throughout this chapter, these segments have the potential to significantly impact the success of any academic writing in terms of publication, readership as well as its accessibility, and consequently, the frequency of it being cited.

REFERENCES

1. James ER. What is an abstract? [cited 2017 May 30]; Available from: http://employees.oneonta.edu/ebertjr/what_is_an_abstract.htm
2. Musa AU, Musa AM, Musa S. An assessment of indexing and abstracting services. Research on Humanities and Social Sciences 2014;4(8):21-9.
3. Caramelli B. Abstract: the trailer of scientific communication, editorial writing and scientific literature. Rev Assoc Med Bras (1992) 2011; 57(6):607.
4. National Information Standards Organization. "Guidelines for Abstracts". ANSII/NISO Standard 1997; Z39(14).
5. Mack C. How to write a good scientific paper: title, abstract, and keywords. J Micro/Nanolith, MEMS MOEMS 2012;11(2).
6. University of Adelaide. Language and learning guide. Writing an abstract. [cited 2017 May 30]; Available from: URL:http://www.victoria.ac.nz/education/pdf/Writing_an_abstract.pdf
7. Soranno. Citing information and scientific writing. 2011 [cited 2017 May 30]; Available from: URL:http://www.soranno.fw.msu.edu/documents/FW472_litcitedguidelines_11.pdf
8. The Writing Center, University of North Carolina at Chapel Hill. [cited 2017 May 30]; Available from: URL:http://writingcenter.unc.edu/handouts/abstracts/
9. Koopman P. How to write an abstract. 1997 October. [cited 2017 May 30]; Available from: URL:https://users.ece.cmu.edu/~koopman/essays/abstract.html
10. Simulation & Gaming An interdisciplinary journal of theory, practice and research. Structured Abstracts. [cited 2017 May 30]; Available from: URL:http://www.unice.fr/sg/authors/abstracts.htm
11. Indiana University. Writing Tutorial Services. Writing Abstracts. [cited 2017 May 30]; Available from: URL:http://wts.indiana.edu/pamphlets/abstracts.shtml

12. Margalit D. Some Dos and Don'ts for Writing Abstracts. [cited 2017 May 30]; Available from: URL:https://people.math.gatech.edu/~dmargalit7/tsr/DosandDontsforAbstracts.pdf
13. Shirley MM. A Dozen Dos and Don'ts: Thoughts after reading hundreds of abstracts. 2010 Ronald Coase Institute. [cited 2017 May 30]; Available from: URL:https://www.coase.org/writings/shirley2010dosanddontsinabstracts.pdf
14. Midwestern State University Guide. How to write a research abstract. [cited 2017 May 30]; Available from: URL:https://mwsu.edu/Assets/documents/eureca/writing-abstracts.pdf
15. Cerejo C. Manuscript Structure. A 10-step guide to make your research paper abstract more effective. [cited 2017 June 6]; Available from: URL:http://www.editage.com/insights/a-10-step-guide-to-make-your-research-paper-abstract-more-effective
16. Joshi Y. Why do journals ask for keywords? 2014 Feb 27. [cited 2017 May 30]; Available from: URL:http://www.editage.com/insights/why-do-journals-ask-for-keywords
17. Panters M. American Journal Experts. Choosing effective keywords. [cited 2017 May 30]; Available from: URL:http://www.aje.com/en/arc/editing-tip-choosing-effective-keywords/
18. Rodrigues V. How to write an effective title and abstract and choose appropriate keywords. [cited 2017 May 30]; Available from: URL:http://www.editage.com/insights/how-to-write-an-effective-title-and-abstract-and-choose-appropriate-keywords
19. Dash M. Three pillars of a biomedical research article: The title, abstract and keywords. J Health Spec [serial online] 2016;186-9. [cited 2017 May 30]; Available from: URL:http://www.thejhs.org/text.asp?2016/4/3/186/186488

CHAPTER

4

Introduction of a Research Paper

Nirmal Chandra Bhattacharyya

The introduction of a research paper is one of the most important task to write. It is basically aimed at giving a brief overview about the topic of research, the rationale of the research work and the context, a brief explanation about the research questions and hypothesis. The length of the introduction will vary depending on the type of research paper, and there is no set standard regarding the ideal length of the introduction. A well-written introduction should be able to attract the reader's interest, encouraging the reader to go through the entire article and critically analyze the content of the article.

According to the IMRAD structure, which is followed universally in writing a research article, the "introduction" is the beginning of the main text of the article after the abstract and keywords. The abbreviation, IMRAD, stands for "Introduction, Methods, Results and Discussion". IMRAD has dominated academic, scientific, and public health journals since the second half of the 20th century. It is recommended in the "Uniform Requirements for Manuscripts Submitted to Biomedical Journals".[1] The IMRAD structure helps to eliminate unnecessary detail and allows relevant information to be presented clearly in a logical sequence.[2,3]

For writing a good introduction, the author should give attention to the following aspects of the research work, which are to be mentioned in brief in the introduction:

ABOUT THE TOPIC OF RESEARCH

Introduction is started with a brief background of the research work, the basic reasons how and why this research question came up, and the probable solutions that can be offered. In general, introduction presents the purpose of the research paper briefly. It provides the readers with a preliminary idea about the content of the article and encourages them to go through the article in detail. It is, therefore, necessary to write about the concept or any new terminology of the research work early in the introduction. This is especially important if a new concept is being introduced with the use of any terminology about which the readers may be unfamiliar with.

ABOUT THE CONTEXT OF RESEARCH

It is necessary to include a very brief review of the existing literature already published in the field. It proves that the author has a strong knowledge and background information of the topic. The author should be able to express the specific areas most relevant to the research topic. It is important that this should be concise and yet able to indicate the author's view on the recent developments in the topic, at the same time, lengthy discussion on the subject should be avoided.

ABOUT THE RATIONALE OF THE RESEARCH WORK

The author should clearly and briefly indicate the value of the research work and its contribution to the subject. In case of medical and public health related subject of research, the author may mention the probable benefit to the community once the proposed hypothesis is proved. In case of experimental work, it is necessary to mention if any experimental models are used in the study.

ABOUT THE RESEARCH QUESTION AND HYPOTHESIS

- The research question is mentioned towards the end of the introduction. It should be brief and focused. It must be able to relate with the title of the paper, and should be able to guide a problem into a testable hypothesis.
- For the development of good research question, FINER (Feasible, Interesting, Nobel, Ethical and Relevant) criteria have been recommended.[3]
- Once the research question is set, a concise and clear statement about the hypothesis should be mentioned. This is a statement which indicates the specific contribution or a result of the study that is likely to emerge from the research work.
- To address the research question, objectives are formulated. The objectives should be Specific, Measurable, Attainable, Realistic and Time bound (SMART).[4]

PARAGRAPHS

For an original research article, three to four paragraphs may be needed for writing the introduction. However, for short review papers and case reports, one paragraph may suffice to introduce the purpose of the study. One approach may be to start with one paragraph that introduces the reader to the field of study. The next paragraph then describes the context and rationale. The third paragraph deals with the research question and hypothesis. Finally, a summary sentence may be added stating how the answer to the research question may contribute to existing knowledge in the subject.[6] However, shortness is the soul of clarity. Detail descriptions, speculations and criticism of other studies may be left for the chapter on discussion.[7]

Thus, the introduction gives a brief review of the research work to be undertaken. It must be realized that the introduction differs from a structured abstract. The structured abstract is the summary of the entire article including the results and conclusion, while the introduction mainly deals with the purpose of the research work.

LIMITATIONS

If there is any weakness in the research work, the introduction is the proper place to mention it in brief. For example, an ideal experiment should have perfectly randomized samples, but if there are some good reasons why this is not possible in the experiment, the readers must be told about this in the beginning with good reasoning, so that they are aware of the shortcomings in the study, and they can be sure about the authenticity of the work.

TIPS FOR GOOD INTRODUCTION

There are few tips that can help a new author to write a good introduction.

- A long introduction with unnecessary details will soon make the reader lose interest in the article. The author must stick closely to the purpose of the paper and structure the introduction methodically.
- The introduction should logically end at the research question and the hypothesis. The reader, after going through the introduction, should be able to know exactly what the author is trying to achieve with the paper. The same will be reflected again during the discussion and conclusion of the study. While reading the article, the reader will be able to correlate the conclusion with the purpose of the study which is already mentioned in the introduction.
- While writing the article, at some stage, the author may feel that the writing in the article has gone in a slightly different direction than initially planned. In this case, the writer may have to adjust the introduction accordingly. Alternatively, the materials and methods, results and discussion may be written first, leaving the introduction to be structured accordingly, so that there is no significant difference between what was originally planned and what conclusions had been drawn at the end of the study.

Examples of Introduction

Original Research Paper

Title: Probiotics for promoting feed tolerance in very low birth weight neonates—a randomized controlled trial.[8]

Introduction

Enteral feeding intolerance is a major issue in premature infants, resulting in prolonged hospitalization and a predisposition to serious complications due to prolonged use of parenteral nutrition. A delay in reaching full enteral feedings is also associated with a poorer mental outcome in preterm neonates at 24 months corrected age.

As the maturation of motor activity in premature infants lags behind that of digestive and absorptive functions, it is most frequently a disorder of gastrointestinal motility that limits the use of enteral feeding in this population. An adequate establishment of the intestinal flora after birth is strictly related to motility maturation and plays a crucial role in the development of gut barrier function and the innate and adaptive immune system.

Enteral supplementation of probiotics prevents severe necrotizing enterocolitis (NEC) and all-cause mortality in preterm infants. Moreover, among the many strategies tried for prevention of feeding intolerance, probiotics are the most promising. However, they are yet to be used as standard of care. The objective of this trial was to determine the efficacy of probiotics on feed tolerance in very low birth weight (VLBW) neonates.

Case Report

Title: Incomplete Miller Fisher syndrome with advanced stage Burkitt lymphoma.[9]

Introduction

Paraneoplastic neurological syndromes (PNS) are rare disorders triggered by an altered immune system response to a neoplasm.

They are defined as clinical syndromes involving nonmetastatic systemic effects that accompany malignant disease. PNS affect less than 0.01% patients with cancer. Small-cell lung cancer, breast cancer and ovarian cancer are the most frequent solid tumors associated with PNS. Hematological malignancies such as non-Hodgkin lymphoma are rarely accompanied by PNS affecting the central and peripheral nervous systems. There are some reports on the association of non-Hodgkin lymphoma and PNS, but Miller Fisher syndrome (MFS) is extremely rare.

REFERENCES

1. International Committee of Medical Journal Editors. Uniform requirements for manuscripts submitted to biomedical journals: writing and editing for biomedical publication. J Pharmacol Pharmacother 2010; 1(1):42-58.
2. Sollaci LB, Pereira MG. The introduction, methods, results, and discussion (IMRAD) structure: a fifty-year survey. J Med Lib Assoc 2004;92(3):364-71.
3. Hulley SB, Cummings SR, Browner WS, Grady DG, Newman TB. Designing clinical research. 3rd ed. Philadelphia: Lippincott Williams and Wilkings; 2007.
4. SMART Objectives. [cited 2017 June 20]; Available from: URL:http://www.health.state.mn.us/divs/opi/qi/toolbox/objectives.html
5. Day RA. The origins of the scientific paper: the IMRAD format. Am Med Writers Assoc J 1989;4(2):16-8.
6. Fisher JP, Jansen JA, Johnson PC, et al. Guidelines for writing a research paper for publication. [cited 2017 May 30]; Available from: URL: https://www.liebertpub.com/media/pdf/English-Research
7. Diane Cooper. How to write an original research paper. [cited 2017 May 30]; Available from: URL:https://www.researchgate.net/publication/275586323_How_to_write_an_original_research_paper_and_get_it_publishedl_Diane_Cooper_AHIP

8. Shashidhar A, Suman Rao PN, Nesargi S, et al. Probiotics for promoting feed tolerance in very low birth weight neonates—a randomized controlled trial. Indian Pediatr 2017;54(5):363-7.
9. Ozdemir ZC, Kar YD, Yarar C, Paylysoy S, Bor O. Incomplete Miller-Fisher syndrome with advanced stage Burkitt Lymphoma. Indian Pediatr 2017;54(5):413-5.

CHAPTER

5

Materials and Methods

Anku Moni Saikia

The backbone of any research protocol/paper is its methodology or materials and methods, which determines the reliability and validity of research. So, utmost care should be taken while writing methodology. The methodology section must be accurate enough to enable the other researcher to replicate the study, but the information must not be overloaded. It must be written in a very direct and precise way, so that it is easily understandable. It must explain all the procedures and activities undertaken to achieve the objectives. It should be kept in mind that the descriptions of unimportant details and basic procedures are to be avoided.

Basic things that need to be mentioned for scientifically sound methodologies are:

1. Study setting
2. Study design
3. Period of study
4. Study area
5. Study population

6. Sample size
7. Sampling technique
8. Study variables
9. Data collection tools
10. Data collection technique
11. Data analysis.

STUDY SETTING

Whether the study is community-based or institution-based should be specifically mentioned in the methodology.

STUDY DESIGN

Understanding of study design is the core of any sound research and, as such, must be mentioned. The study design will depend upon the research questions as well as the resources (time, expertise, personnel, money and logistics). A study may be observational (descriptive or analytical) or experimental (syn. interventional). Descriptive studies may be cross-sectional, case report or case series. Types of analytical studies are case-control, cohort, cross-sectional, and that of experimental are randomized controlled trial (RCT) or clinical trial, field trial and community intervention trial. Following points help in deciding the study design:

- If the research question seeks the answer with regards to frequency or prevalence of any disease, health-related events or states, and distribution of such events in population in terms of time (WHEN they are occurring), place (WHERE they are occurring) and person (WHO are affected), then definitely the study design will be "descriptive" study. There is no control or comparison group in this study design. From this type of study, the researcher is basically trying to find out characteristics with which the particular event or state is associated and accordingly generate the hypothesis.

A cross-sectional descriptive study is done on a cross-section of population at one point of time and has no follow-up. This is basically done to estimate the prevalence or magnitude of a disease, behavior and risk factors (smoking, high fatty diet, etc.) or practices (healthcare utilization, contraceptive use, etc.).

Few examples of cross-sectional descriptive studies are:

a. Prevalence of low birth weight (LBW) among the deliveries in a hospital.
b. Job satisfaction among medical college faculties of Assam.
c. Maternal and child healthcare utilization by the mothers of slum of Guwahati city.

In the above examples, it has been observed that the studies do not seek to prove any causal association between two variables; it simply describes the variables in the population. The researcher can generate hypothesis based on findings of descriptive studies. From the first example (a), the findings may suggest that LBW was significantly more among mothers who had smoked. So, the hypothesis generated may be "Maternal smoking is a cause of low birth weight". However, the hypothesis needs to be more specific regarding the dose and duration of exposure (number of cigarettes per day and duration of smoking).

Case report and case series are not encouraged in the context of evidence-based medicine (EBM) as it occupies the bottom of the hierarchy pyramid of EBM. But it can be an eye-opener for future research and may provide useful information.

- If the aim of study is to establish an association between exposure and outcome variable, or the study starts with a preformed hypothesis, then the design is an "analytical" one. "Exposure" in epidemiological research is the independent variable which is linked to an outcome. "Outcome" is the dependent factor. Change in exposure leads to change in outcome. For instance, if the hypothesis is "intake of alcohol increases the risk of liver cancer", the exposure variable is "alcohol" and outcome variable is "liver cancer". Similarly, in a study on the effect of one particular antihypertensive drug for control of hypertension, exposure variable is the "antihypertensive drug" and "hypertension" is the outcome variable. In other words, exposure is the cause and outcome is the effect. If we want to establish the hypothesis generated in example (a), we have to measure the association between exposure (maternal smoking) and outcome (LBW). In that case, it will be an analytical study. The researcher has to choose the particular analytical study design (case control, cohort, cross-sectional) based on characteristic of the disease concerned and availability of resources.

Case-control study is the type of analytical design where both the exposure (maternal smoking) and outcome (LBW) have already occurred. In this design, we pick up the cases as well as their matched control and comparison is done between the two groups. "Cases" are subjects who have the disease or problems under study. "Controls" are those who do not have the disease in question, but otherwise similar to the cases. History of exposure is collected retrospectively from both the groups. We will encounter four groups here–among cases, some will have exposure to the particular factor, some will not. Again among controls, some will experience the exposure and some will not. If the exposure is significantly more among cases than control group, then the observed difference is not due to chance factor, it is a real difference and hypothesis is accepted. Case control study is done for rare diseases or diseases about which little is known.[1]

In case of some diseases having wider clinical spectrum, "cross-sectional analytical design" has to be adopted.[2] Here, from a "sample population", two groups are identified–one having the disease and other not. Exposure history has to be elicited from all the subjects. Analysis is done between both the groups and their exposure status. This design is, however, inferior to other analytical designs in the hierarchy pyramid of EBM.

"Cohort" study is a longitudinal study where participants are classified based on exposure status and they are followed over a period of time to see the frequency of disease among them. Here, two groups are considered–a "study" group where the subjects have the "exposure" but free from disease, and a "control" group where the subjects have neither the exposure nor the disease. For example, if we want to test the hypothesis that chewing tobacco can cause oral cancer, we start by taking a group of people who are free from oral cancer but have the exposure (E+), i.e. tobacco-chewing habits (study group). Control group is also free from oral cancer and does not have tobacco-chewing habit (E–). Both the groups are equally followed up for development of disease. Here also we will encounter four groups, among "E+", some will develop oral cancer, some will not. Among "E−" subjects, some will develop cancer and some will not. If the oral cancer incidence is significantly more in the "E+" group than "E−" group, the hypothesis is accepted. Cohort study is superior to other analytical and descriptive designs, but it requires more resources. Rare diseases and disease which needs long follow-up are not suitable for cohort study.[1]

- An "experimental" study is intended to see the efficacy of treatment (new drug/procedure), preventive procedure (vaccine) or a healthcare system. In this study, in contrast to other designs, the subjects are followed up to see the outcome after the intervention/manipulation. For a conclusive result, interventional study ought to be an RCT. In this design, the study participants are randomly allocated into two groups–experimental group, receiving the intervention and control group, receiving the placebo/standard treatment. An example is to see whether drug "X" is more effective in controlling diabetes than the conventional hypoglycemic drug "Y". The study group will receive drug "X" and control group will receive drug "Y". Random allocation is followed in selecting the groups to prevent bias. But the groups do not know whether they are receiving new drug or old drug. This is called single-blinding. Sometimes, even the investigator does not know who is getting what. In that circumstance, it is called double-blinding. If drug "X" is found to be more effective in the control of diabetes than drug "Y", the hypothesis is accepted.

In case of interventional studies, mentioning about details of randomization, blinding and follow-up is mandatory.

PERIOD OF STUDY

It indicates the relevance of issue under study. It should be specifically mentioned in the methodology.

STUDY AREA

Some information relevant to study objectives should be mentioned, for example, basic demographic information, existent health services, etc.

STUDY POPULATION

"Reference population" is the population on which the study results will be generalized. On the other hand, "study population" is the population selected from reference population, which is actually participating in the study. Both the populations should be specified categorically.

Inclusion and exclusion criteria of the study population should be precisely defined. Inclusion criteria are the characteristics that the subjects must have to be eligible for the study. Exclusion criteria imply another list of conditions that exclude a subject who is otherwise eligible for the study. The result of the study is likely to be biased if these criteria are not well defined beforehand. The investigator must decide these criteria with utmost care, based on existing scientific information and available literature for the same.

For example, in an RCT for assessing the efficacy of intravenous iron therapy over oral iron therapy in iron-deficiency anemia (IDA) in pregnancy, inclusion criteria must include women in 2nd and 3rd trimesters of pregnancy with peripheral smear suggestive of IDA, and exclude women with severe anemia requiring blood transfusion. If we want to see the prevalence of Alzheimer's dementia in a community-based study, we must exclude the patients with history of stroke or head injury. If it is not done, the prevalence of the disease will come out much more than actual. Informed consent according to Declaration of Helsinki has to be taken.

SAMPLE SIZE

How many study subjects are needed? Are we going to study the whole population or a sample of it? In most of the scientific researches, it is not possible to study the whole population. So, most research studies involve the observation of a sample from the population of interest. Now, the most difficult question in front of a researcher is how large the sample should be. The scientific approach to determine the appropriate sample size depends on how much error can be tolerated as between the real situation in the population and sample results (sampling errors). However, the main determinant of the sample size is study design and measures of outcome variables (rates/means/proportions). Different formulas are used in different situations. For example:

In cross-sectional (prevalence) studies, sample size is calculated by using a simple formula:

$$n = Z^2P(1 - p)/d^2$$

Where n = sample size; Z = statistic for a level of confidence; p = expected prevalence or proportion; d = precision.

Z statistic for the level of confidence of 95%, which is set at 1.96. It means that 95% of normal distribution would lie within ± 1.96 standard deviation of either side of the mean. According to the desired level of confidence of the investigator, the value of Z is chosen.

Prevalence "P" can be taken from previous studies. Studies with similar design and study population and most recent studies would be most preferable for considering "p",[3] else a pilot study can be undertaken. If it is not possible to estimate "p", a figure of 0.5 should be used; this is the safest choice since sample size is required as and when p = 0.5.[4]

Precision "d" is the maximum error in sample size estimate which is acceptable. "d" in the formula should be a proportion of one rather than percentage. There is not enough guidelines for choosing appropriate "d". A common recommendation is to set d = p/2 for rare disease and (1 – p)/2 for common conditions.[3] For finding a suitable sample size, the assumption usually made is that "d" does not exceed 10% or 20% of "p".[5]

Sample size calculation varies with different study designs as well as type of variables. Investigator should consult biostatistician in sample size calculation and sampling technique. But, it is the investigator/researcher who decides the expected confidence limit and precision based on research questions. Nowadays, various computer statistical softwares are available for this purpose. However, no such formula is used in qualitative research.

SAMPLING TECHNIQUE

Once sample size is determined, the next step is how we are going to select the sample from the population? Sampling techniques may be of two types—probability or nonprobability. Probability sampling method is more representative of target population.[6] Which particular method is being adopted and justification for the same is an essential requisite.

We have to have a "sampling frame" for drawing random samples. The sampling frame is the complete list of elements or units of the population. For example, in a community-based study, if we want to study 10 villages from a block, the sampling frame will be the list of all villages under the block. Mentioning of sampling frame is very crucial for sound methodology write-up.

Nonprobability sampling techniques, like convenience sampling, judgmental sampling, etc. are more indicated and used in qualitative research. Random sampling techniques cannot be used in understanding the issues related to human behavior, hence inappropriate in qualitative research.[7] For example, if research question is to see why people are not utilizing the available government health services, this will be under the domain of qualitative research.

STUDY VARIABLES

Variables are characteristics which vary from person to person or object to object. The investigators observe, measure (in observational study), manipulate or control (in interventional study) the variables based on study objectives. The variables may be dependent or outcome, independent or exposure and confounding variables.

Exposure and outcome variables have been described earlier in the chapter. In a hypothesis of "Smoking increases the risk of ischemic heart disease (IHD)", smoking is exposure-variable, IHD is outcome-variable and alcohol is a confounder-variable which is associated with both exposure (smoking) and outcome (IHD), independently. Every effort should be made to control confounder. The methodology section should clearly explain the variables under study and how these variables are measured. Variables need to be defined precisely. For some variable, where standard definitions are not available or are not feasible to adhere to standard definitions, operational definitions have to be made and mentioned. If any categorization like mild, moderate and severe is done for some variables, the cut-off points have to be mentioned. In longitudinal or cohort study, the methods and frequency of measuring the variables have to be decided beforehand.

DATA COLLECTION TOOLS

Tools include different instruments or means used for collecting data. This may be physical instrument (sphygmomanometer), laboratory instrument, and procedures or may be a checklist, or an interview schedule or a questionnaire which are predesigned and pretested. Pretesting of schedule/questionnaire is very crucial to see clarity of the questions, to identify problems in collection of information as well as to see the time required for filling the instrument in real situation. Reference has to be mentioned for using particular tools to justify its use. However, there is no need to explain the basic procedure and instrument. For a new tool, validation in that particular setting is needed. The procedure for validation has to be mentioned briefly. If more than one method is available for measuring a particular variable, the investigator should justify the reason for adopting a particular method. The use of a particular technique or method does not depend only on sensitivity and specificity, but also the acceptability, technical convenience and cost.

The type of tools used depends on type of research (qualitative or quantitative), population to be studied and the availability of resources. The methods of quality control of the measurements have to be decided and mentioned.

DATA COLLECTION TECHNIQUE

In simple terms, it is "how to use the tools". Techniques vary with type of study (quantitative or qualitative). This may be an interview in quantitative research and group discussions, observation, in-depth interview, etc. in qualitative research. Any other information related to training of the investigators, supervision of the activities should be specifically mentioned if the study demands.

DATA ANALYSIS

The statistical test and the package used for data analysis should be decided during planning and specifically mentioned in methodology. There are many statistical tests, but the choice depends on many factors, such as the objective of the study, type of variables and measurement scales used, sample size, number of groups to be compared, number of variables, distribution of the outcome variable, etc.[8] The tests and the probability level must have been mentioned in this section.

REFERENCES

1. Park K. Park's Textbook of Preventive and Social Medicine. 23rd ed. Jabalpur: M/S Banarsidas Bhanot Publishers; 2015. p. 74.
2. Bhalwar R. Textbook of Public Health and Community Medicine. 1st edition. Pune: Department of Community Medicine, Armed Forces Medical College; 2009. p. 165.
3. Naing L, Winn T, Rusli BN. Practical issues in calculating the sample size for prevalence studies. Arch Orofacial Sci 2006;1:9-14.
4. Lwanga S, Lemeshow S. Sample size determination in health studies. A practical manual. WHO; 1991. p. 9.
5. Mahajan BK. Methods inbiostatistics. 8th ed. New Delhi: Jaypee Brothers Medical Publishers (P) Ltd; 2016. p. 117.
6. Elfil M, Negida A. Sampling methods in clinical research: an educational review. Emerg (Tehran) 2017;5(1):e52.
7. Marshall MN. Sampling for qualitative research. Family Practice 1996; 13:522-5.
8. McCluskey A, Lalkhen GA. Statistics III: Probability and statistical tests. Contin Educ Anesth Crit Care Pain 2007;7:167-70.

CHAPTER 6

Results and Observations

Anku Moni Saikia, Hiranya Saikia

This section basically reports or presents the collected data or the findings of the study in different forms like tables, diagrams, graphs, and statements. It is the quantity, quality, and type of data that decides the methods of data presentation. This result section is the mirror of the research questions.

The results should be presented in a logical and simple way. The information shown in this section should be straightforward and factual. It should be organized in such a manner that they answer the research questions. Order of presenting "Result" is to be decided by the Researcher as per the research questions or most important to least important outcome. However, continuity has to be maintained in any case. Generally, the order of presentation in "Method" section is adopted for writing "Result" section.[1] All the results that relate to research question should be provided with details including simple counts and percentages. Caution must be taken so that it is not overloaded with unnecessary information. The chance of publication in a good journal depends on the skill of presenting the key findings in a logical way by using illustrative materials and texts.[2] It basically includes the primary outcome measures as key findings. However, if necessary, secondary outcome measure has to be mentioned in Results section. Placement of "Tables" and "Figures" in the manuscript depends on journal's guidelines. Some journals require it on a separate page, while others not. So, it is very much essential to go through the Author's Guidelines before preparing the "Result" section.

This section should be started with descriptive results. Tables and illustrations are to be inserted in an appropriate format. All mean values must be accompanied by the corresponding standard deviations (SDs). Reporting a confidence interval (CI) for every population parameter became a mandatory prerequisite in modern research.[3,4] It is important to state the name of the statistical test at the time of giving "p" values. It is recommended to report both CI and exact P value instead of reporting only P <0.05 or as P <0.01, etc.[5] The use of the word "Significant" in scientific studies implies statistical significance. If "p" value is given, no need to mention about significance.[1] Some statistical results such as ANOVA, multiple comparisons in ANOVA, logistic regression analysis, etc. should be put in an intelligible table. Caution must be taken so that it is not overloaded with unnecessary information.

While writing "Result" section, care must be taken so that same information is not presented by more than one method. Same data should not be presented by both tables and figures. The researcher must choose the best one to make data readable and understandable.

One should not try to explain or justify any findings in this section. Description, explanation, and interpretation of the findings belong to "Discussion" section. The data and information which appear very clearly in a table or figure should not be repeated in the text. Likewise, information that has been written as a statement should not be repeated in the table or figure. However, one or two key results from each table or figure can be addressed in the text. Consistency of data must be maintained between text and diagrams (table, graph, etc.). "Graphs" are more indicated to show trends. In the text, "Table" is referred as "Table" whereas "Figure" can be abbreviated inside the text as "Fig".[1] However, consistency has to be maintained in using the terms.

When data are presented in tabular or pictorial form in any scientific communication, the following basic things need to follow:

- Tables and Figures should be numbered and should be given a "Title".[6,7] The title should be very clear, precise, and self-explanatory. The title is mentioned on the top in case of "Table" and bottom in case of "Figure". Where necessary, explanatory footnotes should be placed beneath the particular table along with a reference symbol.
- The tables should be so simple and understandable that readers should be able to determine what the table intends to say just by looking at the table.
- Absolute numbers in the text and tables should always be provided if percentage is shown. This helps reviewers to understand wherefrom the derivations are calculated.
- Even a negative result that fails to prove a hypothesis should not be ignored and needs to be documented.

- In case of photomicrographs, the stain used and magnification should be written. For photographs of human subjects, suppression of the eyes is required.[7] However, with consent face or identity of the case can be revealed. High resolution images are preferred in many journals for better printing quality.

Prescribed or minimum number of tables and figures for an original article depends on the particular journal. Likewise the format of table including the font type and size varies with journals. So, author must read carefully the guidelines before writing the paper to a particular journal.

The quality of good result writing is determined by the following facts:

- Whether the data is able to answer the research question?
- Whether the statistical methods and tests mentioned in methodology section are addressed in the result section?
- Whether any interpretation or explanation is given in this section?

The "YES" answer to first two questions and "NO" to last question indicate replicable and quality research.

REFERENCES

1. Labani S, Wadhwa K, Asthana S. Basic approach to data analysis and writing of results and discussion section. MAMC J Med Sci 2017;3:6-15.
2. Kallestinova ED. How to write your first research paper. Yale J Biol Med 2011;84(3):181-90.
3. Curran-Everett D. Explorations in statistics: confidence intervals. Adv Physiol Educ 2009;33(2):87-90.
4. Gardner MJ, Altman DG. Confidence intervals rather than P-values: estimation rather than hypothesis testing. Br Med J (Clin Res Ed) 1986;292(6522):746-50.

5. Binu VS, Mayya SS, Dhar M. Some basic aspects of statistical methods and sample size determination in health science research. Ayu 2014;35(2):119-23.
6. Indrayan A. Basic Methods of Medical Research. 2nd ed. New Delhi, India: AITBS Publishers; 2008. pp. 312-13.
7. Goyal RC. Research Methodology for Health Professionals Including Proposal, Thesis and Article Writing. 1st ed. New Delhi: Jaypee Brothers Medical Publishers (P) Ltd; 2013. p. 260.

CHAPTER

7

Discussion and Conclusion

Dipak Kumar Sarma

Structure of an original research article includes title page, abstract, introduction, methods, results, discussion, conclusions, acknowledgements, references, tables and table captions, and figure and figure captions. Most journals want ethical clearance and conflicts of interest to be declared at the end of conclusion.

The discussion is one of the vital parts of the body of the article. One must be very cautious in writing discussion and usually several attempts are needed to write a proper discussion. One must always remember that the writing style of discussion varies from journal to journal and it is better to check the guidelines before writing it.

Many researchers take time to write the discussion section. For many, writing a discussion is as scary as starting the article.[1,2] Most pertinent question is how to start? At the end of the study, the researcher usually has many unique results and findings on hand. Now it is his/her responsibility to use his/her intellect in interpreting these findings in the backdrop of available literature. Depending on the type of study the discussion differs in length, structure, and shape.

Following some general principles on writing the discussion make the writing easier. If the researcher is aware of these rules he/she feels comfortable in writing this section.[1] While writing discussion, the researcher should always keep in mind the purpose of the study. He/she should place the results in context of his/her research. He/she should explain the meaning of the findings in a scientific manner and try to establish why these meanings are important.[1] No arrogance should be expressed in the discussion. At the same time no condescension or patronization should be done.[1] Discussion is a scientific expression and so there is no role of emotion in it.

Before writing a discussion, one should plan its organization. An outline is to be framed in the mind in a logical manner. There are many methods of doing it. Usually, a cluster map, an issue tree or numbering is prepared beforehand. One can use his/her own creativity for this type of planning by using his own organizational structure.

The writer's block always hinders in making the first move in discussion. There are few methods which can help the writer in overcoming this block. One can start writing first two lines as mirror reflection of what is written in introduction.[1,2] From the introduction section, the writing should zoom from its general perspective to specific research question. Another way of writing, is starting with the summary and then zooming out to research context.[1]

An alternative way of making the first move is to predict and comment on alternative explanations of the results that have been found in the study. Evaluation of these explanations sometimes helps to go through logical steps in the discussion.[1]

It is a known fact that writing the opening paragraph is a challenging part for many writers. If someone overcomes it, writing subsequent paragraphs become easier. Writing these paragraphs depends on the study design. If a hypothesis is formulated in the study design one should discuss the results in a logical manner, either to support or reject the hypothesis.[2]

If a phenomenon is being tried for understanding by studying some of its specific effects, discussion should be written in separate paragraphs depending on results of each effect in the study. For a good discussion, a well-defined goal, described in introduction and the findings that are found in the result section in support of it, is extremely helpful.[2] The best choice in writing discussion is to start with the major results of the study to get an answer of the research question.[1]

In many situations there is more than one objective. One should write discussion by using results of each objective separately to address each objective.

One should always remember the research questions and should not deviate from it in writing the discussion. In some discussion the research question is reminded with brief context and placing an answer to it from the study results.[1,2] It is more important, when researcher uses a number of findings to explain a research question.[1]

The subsequent paragraphs should be written in a systematic way. The researcher should identify his/her relevant, significant, and noteworthy findings of the result for discussion. Frequently, mistakes are done by the researcher in finding out important results.

The researcher may give importance to some findings, but the readers may not find it noteworthy.[1] It is said that the researcher should digest all his/her findings in the study and successfully sort out those that are crucial to the reader. He/she should discuss those findings in the light of relevant literature in relation to his/her study question. He/she should discuss to what extent he/she agrees or disagrees with those findings. He/she should give explanation in a very clear and logical way, in the light of evidence-based relevant literature.[2-4] Possible explanation is to be made when he/she disagrees with some findings found in relevant literature.[3] Any unexpected findings should be discussed.[1] The debatable aspects of the study should be discussed in a logical way.[4] The researcher should comment adequately on all results.[3] The researcher should keep in mind that any data presented during the course of discussion should be there in the result section of the main text.

After the discussion, the researcher should accept or reject the proposed hypothesis mentioned in the study.[2] One should mention how the findings of the study will contribute and get its place in current research.[1-3]

If there is any limitation and drawback of the study, the researcher should discuss about those at the end of discussion. He/she should discuss about the potential weakness of his/her interpretations.[1,2,4] He/she should mention about any potential doubt in the study.[1] Suggestions of further studies in the area of study is advisable where necessary, in terms of study design and methodology.[4]

There are some common rules to be followed. If there are many issues, each issue should be discussed in one place. That particular paragraph should be started with a sentence which addresses the issue. It should be followed by relevant data gained in the study. Researcher's idea should be followed with substantial evidence based literature.[3] He should state it clearly and explain it with defending answers from literature. Conclusion should be made at the end of that paragraph about that particular issue. At this point one should not be opinion biased.[3] It has been clearly stated that discussion should not be misused to state opinions.[4] It is mandatory that all previous studies irrespective of their results, either for or against the results obtained during the study period should be metioned.[3] There should not be any repetition of idea in the discussion.[3] It should be a commentary, not a reiteration of results. Others directly related important relevant issues should be discussed. But, one should be very careful, so that the reader is not tracked into another topic not related with the research question.[4] Similarly, many side issues are found to be emerging during the study, which are not related to the research question. These issues should not be included in the study. Discussion must be made as short as possible and they should be very clear.

There is no paper which is 100% perfect. There are always some limitations in all studies. There is a new trend in asking for more transparency in research paper publishing.[5] One should mention the limitations of the study in brief.[2,5] Many authors are afraid of putting them down as they believe it will cause damage to their paper.[5] Even if limitations are not mentioned, experienced editors and reviewers can easily recognize them. Many a times they ask authors to mention the limitations in their studies. One should check the journal where he is going to publish the article for guidelines. Some journals want that limitations should be discussed throughout the text, not at the end of the article.[5] Limitations should be written in simple language in an unapologetic way.[5] One should not give any excuse for the limitations and should not make a promise in the text that they will not be done in future.[5] Declaring limitations do not show any weakness on the part from the author. In fact it expresses his/her modesty, boldness, honesty, and integrity.[1,5] But this also does not mean that the researcher should end only with problems that overrides the researcher's findings.[1] Possible explanations and suggestions can be made for the solution of the limitations.[1] It helps the reader to decide what is to be learnt and what is to be speculated.

SUMMARY

Some journals require summary at the end of the discussion. According to the journal's requirement, it should be written as a separate section or as a part of discussion at its end. A summary is the gist of the study and it contains "take-home message" for the reader. The researcher should remember that all parts of the abstract should not be included in the study. It can be called as an extended conclusion, which justifies and explains the conclusion of the study.[3] In many journals there is no provision of summary.

CONCLUSION

Most of the journals require conclusion at the end of the body of the text. In this section, the work should be introduced very precisely stating the major results. Similarly, most important points in discussion are mentioned very precisely and specifically. The concluding statement should mention about contribution of the study to the existing knowledge.

Some researchers end their articles with a note "more research is needed" at the end of the article. If it is done, one should be specific in pointing out the area where work is needed and the possible hypothesis on which it should be based.[5]

A researcher should remember a few points when writing the conclusion. He/she should not make any statement or draw any conclusion which is not supported by his/her study design and results. Conclusions should have link with the aim of his study.[4] If the researcher puts any recommendation, it should be appropriate and it must not go beyond the limits of his study. If there is a justification, the researcher may put a new hypothesis.[4]

Some journals do not ask for conclusion as a separate section in submission. In such situations, a paragraph should be added at the end of the discussion about "take-home messages" of the study.[1] Depending on the study pattern, a precise and specific statement can be made by mentioning an answer to the research question and its implications on the existing knowledge.[1]

Some journals use a section where result is joined with discussion. In this type of writing, results are immediately followed by interpretation. For examples, Journal of Experimental Medicine and Journal of Clinical Investigation use this type of joint results/discussion section.[1]

REFERENCES

1. Kallestinova ED. How to write your first research paper. Yale J Biol Med 2011;84(3):181-90.
2. Fisher JP, Jansen JA, Johnson PC, et al. Guidelines for writing a research paper for publication. [Internet] 2015. [cited 2017 May 25]; Available from: URL:https://www.liebertpub.com/media/pdf/English-Research-Article-Writing-Guide.pdf
3. Shokeir AA. How to write a medical original article: Advice from an Editor. Arab J Urol 2014;12(1):71-8.
4. Kotur PF. How to write a scientific article for a medical journal. Indian J Anaesth 2002;46(1):21-5.
5. Phil L. How to write a scientific paper for a peer reviewed journal. In: Babor TF, Stenius K, Savva S, O'Reilly, Editors. Publishing addiction science: a guide for the perplexed. 2nd ed. United Kingdom: Multi-Science Publishing Company Ltd; 2008. p. 70.

CHAPTER 8

Author Declaration

Putul Mahanta

Author declaration is one of the most important parts of a manuscript submission which includes submission of ethical clearance letter, declaration of conflict of interest, copy right form, etc. For all most every medical journal author declaration is considered to be mandatory. This part of an author submission along with the manuscript in medical writing covers a number of ethical and legal issues.

CORRESPONDING AUTHOR

The name, affiliation with address, phone number/s, and email address of the corresponding author is very much essential to submit. As the corresponding author is fully responsible for the submission of manuscript over the journal's submission process his contact details are essential. Though not mandatory the same information of the co-authors should also be submitted. However, submission of affiliation and designation of co-author/s are mandatory. However, this guideline varies from journal to journal.

REDUNDANT OR DUPLICATE PUBLICATION

The paper that has already been published more than once without adequate acknowledgment of the source or cross-referencing is called redundant or duplicate publication.

In redundant publication the same data may be presented in more than one publication without referencing, particularly when this is done in such a way that reviewers or readers are unlikely to realize that most or all the findings have been published before. This practice of duplicate publication without notice to the editor carries lots of legal and ethical issues. It may even lead to editorial action ranging from warning to banning of the author from future submission, etc. Widespread publicity of his research misconduct may also be given to many other journals.[1]

When submitting a paper, the author should always make a full disclosure along with the submission about all previous papers that might be regarded as redundant or duplicate publication of the same. It is also the duty of an author to alert the editor, if the work includes subjects about which a previous paper has been published. Relevant copies of such material, including papers in press, should be included with the manuscript to assist the editor in defining how to handle the matter.[2]

AUTHORSHIP

All the contributing author/s should sign the author declaration form or paper. Whoever designated as authors and qualify accordingly should be listed there on. All the authors should take the responsibility for appropriate portions of the content they contributed. The corresponding author however should take the responsibility for the integrity of the work as a whole, from inception to published article.[2]

What to Declare?

- Should declare about their contribution at individual level, so that it does not infringe any copy right of the previous authors.
- Should declare that the article has not been published either whole or any part of it somewhere else, and it is not under consideration for publication.
- Should declare that the entire author has taken the responsibility as they have contributed sufficiently in the article.
- Should declare that all author/s have reviewed the article before submission of manuscript and approved accordingly for publication.

It is also important to mention the individual role of each author mentioned in the manuscript. The information, like who conceived, who designed the study, who has collected and analyzed the data, and who has done the statistical analysis part, etc., should be mentioned.

The entire author has to accept the order of authorship prior to submission to journal for publication. Authorship credit should be given on the basis of his/her contribution to the study. Some mandatory aspects to declare are: Considerable contributions to conception and design—

- Collection of data, its analysis, and interpretation
- Compiling of the article

- Critical review for important intellectual content
- Approval of the article for publication of final version.

Conflict of Interest[3]

Conflict of interest of an author for a given manuscript may exist when an author has ties its activities that could wrongly influence his/her judgment. Financial relationships with an industry are usually considered to be the most important conflicts of interest.

When submitting a manuscript authors are responsible for recognizing and disclosing financial and other conflicts of interest that might bias toward their work. They should acknowledge in the manuscript all financial support for the work and other financial or personal connections to the work. If there are no such conflicts or financial support to acknowledge, the authors should write "None declared" in the column of conflict of interest.

Ethical Issues

Study where "Clinical Drug Testing (CDT)" was done the author/s should declare whether the existing rules for in accordance of rule of land besides international treaties, if any involving human or animal as research participant (RPs) was followed or not. Central Drug Controller approval is also important in those issues.

Research involving human subjects as research participant, authors needs to mention whether the procedures followed were in accordance with the ethical standards of the responsible committee on human experimentation (institutional or regional) and with the

Helsinki Declaration of 1975, as revised in 1983.[2] However, details of it should be best done as a statement in Materials and Methods section.

Human Rights and "Code of Ethics"

As per human and animal right is concern "The Code of Ethics" of the World Medical Association which is known as "Declaration of Helsinki" and ICMR guidelines are very much relevant to be followed by the author in any research or experiments involving humans and animal as participant.[4]

Acknowledgments

Any other contributors who do not come under the authorship criteria, but contributed the technical help, writing assistance, or has provided the departmental chair should be listed in the acknowledgments. Financial and material support should also be recognized here.

Patient Consent

Informed consent of patient is mandatory to declare here, if the paper contains information or image(s) pertaining to an individual patient that could reveal his privacy or become the patient identifiable.

Author needs to declare that written informed consent of the patient or the research participant to publish his photos have been obtained. In a case of a minor requires the explicit consent of the parent or guardian.[5] However, if his/her identity is not disclosed or blurred consent is not required.

Copyright

Submission of paper implies that the paper has not been published before nor it is under consideration for publication in another journal.

Different journals have different policies against the copy right transfer issue, but in most of the cases the author/s needs to sign it before it gets published.[6]

REFERENCES

1. COPE. Redundant publication. [cited 2017 June 10]; Available from: URL:https://publicationethics.org/category/keywords/redundant-publication
2. Elsevier. Mandatory author declaration. [cited 2017 May 30]; Available from: URL:https://www.elsevier.com/__data/promis_misc/JBMTauthor_declaration.pdf
3. SCRIBD. Mandatory author declaration. [cited 2017 June 2]; Available from: URL:https://www.scribd.com/document/259476282/JBMTauthor-Declaration-450E-Alex
4. Elsevier. Guide for Authors. Human and animal rights. [cited 2017 May 30]; Available from: URL:https://www.elsevier.com/journals/preventive-medicine/0091-7435/guide-for-authors
5. BJM case reports. Patient consent. [cited 2017 May 30]; Available from: URL:http://casereports.bmj.com/site/about/guidelines.xhtml
6. ACS Publication. Guidelines for authors. Instruction to author. 2014. [cited 2017 June 1]; Available from: URL:http://pubs.acs.org/paragonplus/submission/nalefd/nalefd_authguide.pdf
7. BMJ Case Reports. Instruction for authors. [cited 2017 June 1]; Available from: URL:http://casereports.bmj.com/site/about/guidelines.xhtml

CHAPTER 9

Reference and Citing: A Brief Discussion

AJ Patowary

Any scientific writing is not complete if the source of the different comments that has been incorporated in the article is not duly referred. Reference or the bibliography is the part of the scientific article which can give the reader the information about the source of the information mentioned in the article. So, though it is the end of the article, many a time becomes the most important part of the article for the reader as by going through it one can trace the similar works done in the field by different authors. Therefore, without the reference, bibliography or citing, a scientific writing is incomplete.

Reference, bibliography or citing are the terms used as synonyms many a time, though all are having its own position in any scientific writing. However, all these terms give information about the books, journals or any other source which were considered or consulted while writing the scientific writing, so that, the readers can clear their doubt if any by going through those books, journals or other sources mentioned in the article.

Any reference, bibliography or citing must contain few things common like the name of the author/s, title of the article, name of the journal or book, when published with name of the publisher and the place of publication, etc., depending up on the source used for easy search and access.

DEFINITION

Different sources have different definitions for defining the terms:
Cambridge dictionary defines as:

- A list of the books and articles that have been used by someone when writing a particular book or article.[1]

Dictionary.com defines as:

- A complete or selective list of works compiled upon some common principle, as authorship, subject, place of publication or printer.
- A list of source materials that are used or consulted in the preparation of a work or that are referred to in the text.
- A branch of library science dealing with the history, physical description, composition and classification of books and other works.[2]

REFERENCE VERSUS BIBLIOGRAPHY: ARE THEY SYNONYMS?[3-5]

As already mentioned, though all these terms are used as synonyms, they are having their own meaning and place in any scientific writings.

Reference

It is the detailed description of the documents used for obtaining the information while writing an article or book, etc.

It is the detailed list of the items that have been used or read and *specifically referred to (or cited) in the article*, and have been enlisted of the sources at the end of the article *maintaining a chronological pattern*.

Bibliography

It is a *list of everything that one gone through while writing any scientific writing, whether or not one have referred specifically to it, maintaining an alphabetical pattern*.

A bibliography can give an overview of the documents by which authors have been influenced while preparing an article even if it is not specifically cited within the article.

Citing

It is an acknowledgment toward the original author or the source of the piece of information from which the information has been obtained while writing the article and it is done within the text of the article or book, the document.

It is usually done as a number denoting the referred document as superscript, subscript or with bracket at the end of the line, depending upon the requirement of the particular journal where it is intended to be published.

IMPORTANCE OF REFERENCING

Referencing or the bibliography is an integral part of any scientific writing; it not only helps the readers, but also essential for the following reasons:

- To acknowledge the work of the original author used while writing the article. It is kind of recognition toward the work of the original author by which the author has been inspired or guided while writing the article.
- To enable the readers to trace the original article which has been cited so that the readers can clear their doubt if any, by going through those articles and also have a chance for further reading in the concerned subject.
- To make the work more informative as the readers can not only go through all the information cited in the articles, but also can have many more while reading those cited articles as cross reference.
- To give credibility to an argument presented in the article.
- To prevent the *plagiarism*, as any work of someone cannot be used in any article without giving due credit to the original author.

WHAT AND WHEN TO BE CITED

Before stating an article, one should go through any related articles or any other piece of information, related to the topic of discussion and prepare the list of the reference and bibliography, identify the references and categorize them in to book, journals, etc.

Source may be:

- Book—in the form of any chapter or part of it
- Journal
- Newspaper or magazine
- Conference paper or proceedings
- Annual report

- Institutional or government publication
- Electronic sources—website, CD-ROM, and databases
- Theses, reports, unpublished works, etc.
- Any communication with someone
- Anything that have been used in the article, borrowed or copied from data published or presented in a public domain which is outside the realm of common knowledge.

ELEMENTS OF THE REFERENCE[3-9]

Any bibliography or referencing cannot become complete without a few elements which are essential to identify the article or the piece of document that has been used in writing the article.

The following are the elements that are to be mentioned in the referencing or bibliography:

- Name/names of author/authors
- Title of document
- When published date or year
- Place of publication (name of publisher in books)
- Edition
- Periodicity (volume/issue/part number)
- Series/page number, etc.

REFERENCING SYSTEMS/STYLES[3-9]

There are many referencing styles used in various journals or books and it depends entirely up on the editorial board or the principle adopted by the publisher of that book or the journal for which the article has been prepared; so it is better to clarify the same before beginning the article.

Table 9.1: Different types of referencing style

Abbreviation	*Full form*
ACS	American Chemical Society
AGLC	Australian Guide to Legal Citation
AMA	American Medical Association
AMJ	Academy of Management Journal Style
APA	American Psychological Association
Chicago	Chicago Manual of Style
CSE (CBE)	Council of Science Editors/Council of Biology Editors
Harvard	Originated in Harvard Medical School, also known as parenthetical referencing
IEEE	Institute of Electrical and Electronics Engineers
MLA	Modern Language Association of America
Vancouver	Vancouver reference style or the author-number system

Different types of referencing are mentioned in Table 9.1.[4]

- However, in most of the journals or books in India and also other countries use the Vancouver reference style, and the same has been discussed in this article.
- In the Vancouver Style, while citing any reference within the text of the article, the reference is identified by Arabic number assign to it and is within round bracket. This applies to references in text, tables, and figures, e.g. (2) and this is the style used

by the referencing software as EndNote, though, some prefers superscript while referencing.

- The number is assigned to each reference in Vancouver system and is to be mentioned as it is cited even if the author(s) is named in the sentence or text.
    - Example: Smith (10) has argued that….
- While citing the same reference again and again, the original number assigned to the reference may be reused in the text, though its position may be different in previous citations in the text.
- While citing multiple references for the same thing in the text, instead of mentioning all the numbers, a hyphen is used to join the first and last numbers that are inclusive or else, commas (without spaces) are used to separate numbers in multiple citations. So, while citing the citations (2,3,4,5 and then 7 and 10), the abbreviated form (2-5,7,10) is used. Please note that hyphen is used to mention the citation numbers which are in continuation but for mentioning only two citations which are in continuation, hyphen is not used, e.g. 1,2.
- While placing the citation numbers within text one should carefully consider the position of the numbers; for example a particular reference may be relevant to only part of a sentence. Usually, the placement of the reference numbers should be outside full stops and commas and inside colons and semicolons; though this may vary according to the requirements of a particular journal or publisher.

Example:

Cosmetic autopsy incision is useful for exploration of the deep-seated hidden injuries particularly in the back (1-4).

In the above example, the different sources where the cosmetic autopsy incision has been described are cited; the different references are shown below.

Reference from a Book

Example:

Name of the author with title first followed by abbreviated first name and middle name without gap followed by full stop

Name of the book with a space at the beginning, capitalized first letter and rest all in small, full stop at the end

1. Mahanta P. Modern text book of forensic medicine and toxicology. New Delhi: Jaypee Brothers Medical Publishers (P) Ltd.; 2014. p. 200-15.

Place of publication with a space at the beginning, followed by colon and then space

Name of the publisher followed by semicolon

Year of publication with a space at the beginning, followed by a full stop, space then "p"full stop, space page numbers, then full stop.

From Chapter of a Book

All the rest part is same as the above, only difference is that, the description of the book is started with "In: then name of the author or the editor of the book; the editor of the book is denoted by mentioning as "editor" after the name.

Example:

Name of the author with title first followed by abbreviated first name and middle name without gap followed by full stop

Name of the chapter (.) space"In"(:) space name of the author of the book with his role in the book like "editor" if any; if no editor is there, only mention the name of author of the book."." space and then name of the book with capitalizes first letter.

2. Patoway AJ. Autopsy. In: Mahanta P, editor. Modern text book of forensic medicine and toxicology. New Delhi: Jaypee Brothers Medical Publishers (P) Ltd; 2014. p.199-215.

Name of the publisher followed by semicolon, then after space year of publication, space then "p" full stop space, followed by page number/s with full stop

Place of publication (:) space

While citing a book, if it is the first edition, then no need to mention the edition, or else have to mention the edition of the book after the name of the book.

Example: Mahanta P. Modern text book of forensic medicine and toxicology, 2nd ed. New Delhi: Jaypee Brothers Medical Publishers (P) Ltd.; 2014. p. 200-15.

More than one author:

If, there is more than one author, the names of all are mentioned with surname first and then abbreviated first name, up to six authors and then put et al.

Up to six authors:

Example: Author name I, Author name II, Author name III, Author name IV, Author name V, Author name VI. Modern text book of forensic medicine and toxicology. New Delhi: Jaypee Brothers Medical Publishers (P) Ltd; 2014. p. 199-215.

More than six authors:

Example: Author name I, Author name II, Author name III, Author name IV, Author name V, Author name VI, et al. Modern text book of forensic medicine and toxicology. New Delhi: Jaypee Brothers Medical Publishers (P) Ltd; 2014. p. 199-215.

Referencing from Journal Article

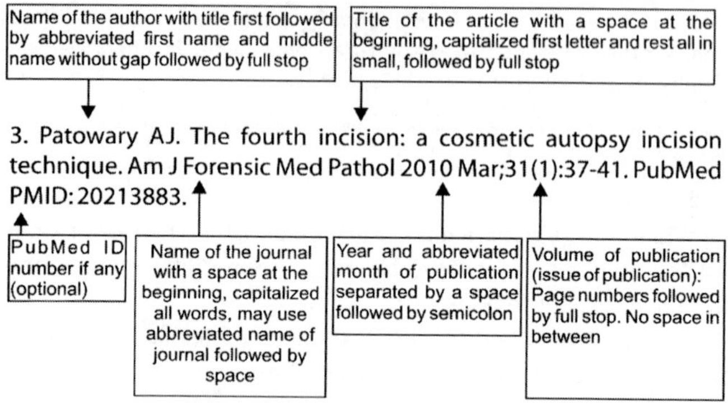

Referencing from Internet Content

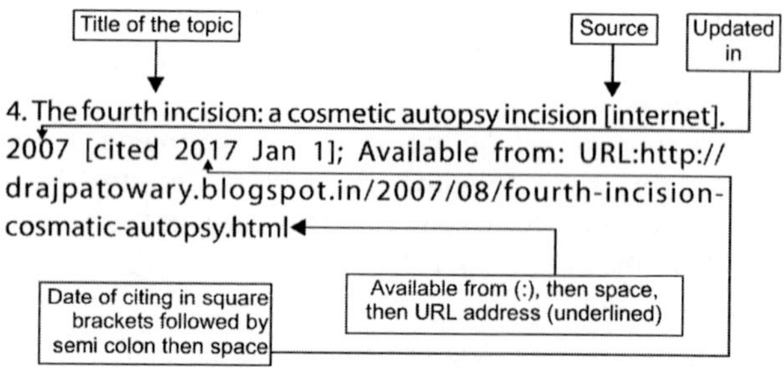

Reference from Dictionary

Example: Dorland's pocket medical dictionary. 23rd ed. New Delhi: Oxford & IBH Publishing Co. Pvt. Ltd; 1983. Autopsy; p. 84

Here the search is for "Autopsy".

Organization as Author

If the article or the reference is taken from some write-up or booklet or any other material published by an organization, the following is followed.

Example: Harvard referencing for the Robert Gordon University. Principles of referencing with examples of references for: books journal articles conference papers web pages. 2010 Aug.

If name of the author is absent:

If the name of the author is not mentioned like in same editorial, the following is followed.

Example: Coffee drinking and cancer of the pancreas [Editorial]. BMJ 1981; 283: 628.

Conference Papers

Example: Patowary AJ. Cosmetic autopsy incision-proposed modification in autopsy incision. In: Das KC, Editor. Scientific bulletin. 1st *Eastern* Zonal Conference of Forensic Medicine & Toxicology; 2006 Dec 8-10; Guwahati, Assam. Guwahati: 2006:82-3.

Conference Proceedings

Example: Vivian VL, editor. Child abuse and neglect: a medical community response. Proceedings of the First AMA National Conference on Child Abuse and Neglect; 1984 Mar 30-31; Chicago. Chicago: *American* Medical Association, 1985.

Scientific or Technical Report

Example: Akutsu T. Total heart replacement device. Bethesda (MD): National Institute of Health, National Heart and Lung Institute; 1974 Apr. Report No. NIH-NHLI-69-2185-4.

Dissertation or Thesis

Example: Ind J Aerospace Med 47(1), 2003 86 Cairns RB. Infrared spectroscopic studies of solid oxygen (dissertation). Berkeley, Univ. of California: 1965.

Newspaper Articles

Example: Barman C. Heavy school bag. The Assam Tribune 2017 Jun 4; 6(col. 3).

ADDITIONAL NOTES ON THE VANCOUVER STYLE

References should be typed single-spaced on separate page(s) and numbered consecutively in the order in which they are cited in the text as superscript and after the full stop. Unpublished work should not be included in the list of references. There is no guideline for the numbers of references to be quoted in a scientific paper, which varies journal to journal. However, a case article should have a minimum of 15, review article 20 and original article 25 references. In the list of references the references should be numbered manually, bullet numbering should be avoided.[10]

Tables

- Each table should be given a brief title.
- Number each table in the text in consecutive order.
- *Explanatory matter is placed in footnotes, not in the heading.*

Illustrations and Figures

- Number each figure in the text in consecutive order.
- The legends should be labeled with numerals corresponding to the figures, etc.
- *The original source if any should be acknowledged.*

Measurement

- Length, height, weight, and volume should be reported in metric units.
- Temperatures should be in degrees Celsius.
- Blood pressure measured in mm of mercury.
- All hematological and biochemistry measurements stated in SI units.

Referencing Tools/Software

As in all other fields, the use of software is making the job of referencing also easier; an author can use any of the software in finalizing the reference. One have to keep in mind that the software can prepares the reference as per the style opted, but the selection of the reference is to be made by the author only.

The following are the software most commonly used for preparing the references:

- Connotea
- CiteULike
- Citation Machine
- Zotero
- EndNote.

In most of them, one can assign the system of referencing is to be followed as per the need and can get the bibliography or reference for the article or the other type of writing; it all depends on the requirement of the agency for which the article is being written. Moreover, after collecting and placing the references in the stipulated area in the software, one can change the referencing type whenever required and whenever there is need to insert the reference in the text, the required reference can be inserted as number mentioned above.

The references can also be generated from the web along with all the data required to complete the reference by the software automatically and is arranged as per the style of reference assigned or if the same is not available in the web, the required panes are to be filled up by the author and the reference is generated by the software.

REFERENCES

1. Cambridge dictionary. Meaning of "bibliography" in the English Dictionary. [Internet] [cited 2017 June 3] Available from: URL:http://dictionary.cambridge.org/dictionary/english/bibliography
2. dictionary.com. Define Bibliography at Dictionary [Internet] [cited2017 June 3]; Available from: URL:http://www.dictionary.com/browse/bibliography
3. Thakur CS, Dhankhar SS, Sengupta AK. A case report on ejection with psychological analysis-Guidelines for Authors. Ind J Aerospace Med 2003;47(1):84-7.
4. International Committee of Medical Journal Editors. Uniform requirements for manuscripts submitted to biomedical journals. Can Med Assoc J 1995;152(9):1462-64.
5. The University of Queensland. Reference/bibliography-Vancouver style. [cited 2017 June 3]; Available from: URL:https://web.library.uq.edu.au/research-tools-techniques/referencing/referencing-style-guides
6. Mauch JE, Park N. Guide to the successful thesis and dissertation a handbook for students and faculty. 5th ed. New York: Marcel Dekker; 2003. p. 138, 139, 141, 207.
7. Harvard referencing for the Robert Gordon University. Principles of referencing with examples of references for: books journal articles conference papers web pages. 2010 Aug.
8. Murray R. How to write a thesis. 2nd ed. Berkshire: Open University Press; 2006.
9. Smith JU, Murrel G, Harold E, et al. Research in medicine planning a project—writing a thesis. 3rd ed. New York: Cambridge University Press; 2010.
10. IJHRMLP. References. [cited 2017 June 2]; Available from: URL:http://www.ijhrmlp.org/instruction_to_author.php

CHAPTER

10

How to Write a Case Report?

Junu Devi

In scientific literature, case report means description of a particular case. Although, evidence from clinical research is usually population based, case-based observations continue to influence our teaching and practice. People love stories and messages can be conveyed easily by storytelling. The most obscure clinical pearl can be made memorable, if narrated in relation to a real event or actual patient.[1] The act of recording the findings and the clinical observation of a patient, discussing this with colleagues and publishing in a journal remains essential to the art of medicine—as Sir William Osler said "Always note and record unusual, publish it, place it on permanent record as a short concise note. Such communications are always of value".[2]

THE IMPORTANCE OF A CASE REPORT

Case reports and case series (collection of individual case reports which may occur within a short period of time) are types of studies in which an unusual feature of a disease or in case of case series, different factors in the history and investigation of the individual cases can lead to formulation of a hypothesis which can further be tested by analytical studies. The cases with documented unusual medical reports may represent the first clue in identification of a new disease or adverse effect of some exposure. Sometimes these case reports may represent the emergence of a new epidemic.[3] For example, Parkinson's disease and HIV-related acquired immune deficiency syndrome were first described in the case study format.

Some essential pieces of information, undetected or missed in clinical trials, can be gathered from published case reports. This format remains an important means of increasing clinical insight and enhancing our knowledge base.[4]

DEFINITION OF CASE REPORT

"A case report is a detailed report of the symptoms, signs, diagnosis, treatment, and follow-up of an individual patient. Case report may contain a demographic profile of the patient, but usually describe an unusual or novel occurrence. Some case reports also contain a literature review of other reported cases."[5] It is a means of communicating information that has been gathered from clinical practice, this could be an unusual or previously unknown condition, a rare presentation or complication of a known disease or even a different approach to managing a common condition.[6]

THE NEED TO WRITE A CASE REPORT

Many authors agree that the case reports have their place in the published literature and they should be written because they provide new knowledge to the field of healthcare.[7-10] Case remains as one of the few ways to bring in a new condition or new etiology to the attention of the scientific community.[11,12]

Other reasons are: (1) Case reports are educational and interesting for students and authors.[13,14] (2) The evidence base regarding a condition may be increased when practitioners report unique cases from their clinical practice.[15-17]

There are three types of case reports—diagnostic case reports, management case reports, and educational case reports. *Diagnostic case reports* describe and discusses the diagnostic and analytic methods used to evaluate a patient. These cases present a diagnosis that is rare, confusing or difficult to arrive at but management part is not discussed.[9,18] *Management case reports* describe the full management aspect of a patient. *Educational case reports* provide a brief review of literature along with diagnostic and management parts of the case.[19]

Literature search: Thorough literature search using PubMed, Ovid, Medline, Embase, and Google Scholar should be done.[6] Previously published case reports will improve understanding of the topic, and give ideas for unique message for a case report. By reading the literature one may be able to educate consultants with the latest evidence.

Collate the information: Starting from detailed history, examination findings, reports of investigations, management (including operative findings), and outcome of the patient should be systematically collected and recorded.[6]

Limitation of the case report: Findings of a case cannot be generalized beyond the context of the particular patient.[17,20,21] One can never conclude, based on the observation of a single patient, whether any particular management strategy effective in a select case will be equally effective for other patients with the same condition.[22] However a hypothesis can be generated based on a case report which can later be tested using experimental clinical trials.[19]

WRITING THE MANUSCRIPT

Case reports should not be very long. The word limit may vary from journal to journal. As recommended by Cohen word limit should be between 1,500 and 2,500 words.[4] However, Sorinola et al.[8] found words restriction to be between 500 and 2,000 words with a median of 1,000 words. Authors should verify that the length of the case report is within the word limit recommended by the journal in question as mentioned in the guide to authors.[19] It is important that the author delivers a single message through the case report.

The format adopted for most case reports:

1. *Title*: The title should be clear concise, and should have accurate description of the patient, under study. Abbreviations within the title should always be avoided.
2. *Abstract*: Abstract should be short. It summarizes the case presentation and message of the report. Abstract should be around 150–200 words.[6] It should not cross 350 words.[23] Abbreviations or references within the abstract should not be used. The abstract should be structured in the three sections: Background—an introduction about why this case is important. Case presentation—brief detail of the case along with

demographic detail. Discussion and Conclusion—what the reader should learn from the case report and what the clinical impact will be.

Keywords: This section comprises of 3–10 keywords representing the main content of the article.

3. *Introduction*: Introduction needs to introduce subject matter of the case, to the reader. It should explain the background of the case including disorder, usual presentation and progression, and an explanation of the presentation, if it is a new disease. It should also include brief literature review.[23] Information from a review of the literature allow the authors to relate the context of this case in relation to previously published data.[15,16] Introduction should include how rare the condition is and why the case report is important. Introduction should not be too lengthy. Always try to write down three particular parts: (1) what we know; (2) what we do not know, and (3) why we have reported the case (what is being reported in the article). Introduction should be between 100 and 150 words, but definitely not more than 500 words in any case. A crisp introduction with a good language create interest in the reader.[24]
4. *Case Presentation*: The case should be described in a concise and chronological order, which is enjoyable to follow. One should usually begin with the history, examinations findings, investigation, and treatment in that order without the headings.[6] There should be enough detail (but not too much) for the reader to establish his or her own conclusion about the validity. Superfluous or confusing information should be avoided.[4] Photograph or illustration of diagnostic procedure and radiograph can

also be helpful in conveying a clear message to the reader and should be used when appropriate. Inferences of the case report and its management should be saved for the discussion section.

5. *Discussion*: Discussion is written by briefly expanding the introduction, explaining why our particular case is important and of interest to the reader.[6] It should evaluate the accuracy, validity, and uniqueness of the case; compare and contrast the case report with current published literature with contemporary references.[4,23] Authors should focus on what is learnt from the present case, what has already been reported in the literature about the condition, and what main hypothesis and theories used to explain the clinical findings. Main differential diagnosis is discussed in this section. Finally, author should describe in detail the messages that are conveyed through the case report and some suggestions for future enquiry into the topic.[6,16]
6. *Conclusion*: The conclusion should contain the primary take home message avoiding repetition. It includes the perspective for areas of possible improvement with similar case study in future. It helps the reader in understanding the main motive of the manuscript. This section gives the author a chance to have the last word on the subject. Make sure your last word counts![24]
7. *Abbreviations*: When abbreviations are used in the text they should be defined in the text at first use, and a list of abbreviations can be provided.
8. *Consent*: This section is compulsory for most of the journals. Already discussed in the previous chapter 9.
9. *Conflict of Interest*: Already discussed in the previous chapter 9.
10. *Author Contribution*: Already discussed in the previous chapter 9.

11. *Author Information*: This may include details about the author's qualifications, current position they hold at institutions or societies, or any other relevant background information.[23]
12. *Acknowledgement*: Already discussed in the previous chapter 9.
13. *References*: Authors should search for and cite published case reports that are relevant to the case they are presenting. Usually, there should be no more than 15 references.[23] However some journals impose limits on the number of references allowed for case reports.[4,13] References should be formatted appropriately as described in the journal's instructions for authors.[19]
14. *Tables*: Tables are self-contained, need no text to support them. They should have a corresponding title. Permission should be obtained from the publisher to reprint a previously published table.[19]
15. *Figures*: Figures are self-contained, need no text to support them. Permission to reprint a previously published figure is obtained from the publisher. Written permission to publish photos of models or identifiable people is obtained. Figures are prepared according to the journal's instructions to authors.[19]

SUBMITTING THE CASE REPORT

Once the author has completed the first draft, spelling and grammar should be checked. Proofreading and final revision should be done by coauthors or with the help of some seniors. A covering letter should be prepared to accompany the article. Be aware, that you cannot submit your article to a second journal, whilst awaiting a decision from the first.

CONCLUSION

Case reports are first line of evidence documenting clinical phenomenon in the peer reviewed literature. Proper preparation of a case report is necessary for it has to be published. Before submitting one should go through final check list. Case report should be clear, concise, and coherent and should convey an appropriate message.

REFERENCES

1. Friedman JN. The case for... writing case report. Paediatr Child Health 2006;11(6):343-4.
2. Thayer WS. Osler, the teacher Sir William Osler, Bart. 1920, Baltimore: Johns Hopkins Press. pp. 51-2.
3. Ranadeb Biswas, editor. A Hand Book on Biostatistics. Indian Association of Preventive and Social Medicine. West Bengal Chapter Kolkata: West Bengal; 2008.
4. Cohen H. How to write a case report. Am J Health Syst Pharm 2006; 63(19):1888-92.
5. Case Report. [cited 2017 Junu 12]; Available from: URL:http://en.wikipedia.org/wiki/Case_report
6. Kirthi Varo. How to write a Clinical case report. RCP insight/ Royal college of Physicians. 2011. [cited 2017 Junu 12]; Available from: URL:http://rcplondon.ac.uk
7. Janicek M. Clinical case reporting in evidence based medicine. Oxford: Butterworth-Heinemann; 1999.
8. Sorinola O, Olufwobi O, Coomarasamy A. Instructions to authors for case reporting are limited: a review of a journal list. BMC Med Educ 2004;4:4.
9. Keating JC. Towards a philosophy of the science of chiropractic: a primer for clinician. Stockton, CA: Stockton Foundation for Chiropractic research; 1992. pp. 199-222.
10. Walter G, Rey JM, Dekker F. The humble case report. Aust N Z J Psychiatry 2001;35:240-5.

11. Vandenbrouke JP. Case report in an evidence-based worlds. J R Soc Med 1999;92:159-62.
12. Godlee F. Applying research evidence to individual patients. BMJ 1998;316:1621-2.
13. Fenton JE. Khoo SG, Ahmed I, et al. Tackling the case report. Auris Nasus Larynx 2004;31:205-7.
14. Pierson DJ. Case report in respiratory care. Respir Care 2004;49:1186-94.
15. Croll TP. Preparation of a dental case history report for publication. J Am Dent Assoc 1981;102:59-61.
16. DeBakey L, DeBakey S. The case report. I. Guidelines for preparation. Int J Cardiol 1983;4(3):357-64.
17. Doherty M. What value case reports? Ann Rheum Dis 1994;53:1-2.
18. Kratochwill TR, Levin JR. Single-case research design and analysis: New direction for psychology and education. Hillsdale NJ: Lawrence Erlbaum Associates; 1992. p. 1-14.
19. Green BN, Johnson CD. How to write a case report for publication. J Chiropr Med 2006 Summer;5(2):72-82.
20. Martyn C. Case reports, case series and systematic reviews. Q J Med 2002;95:197-8.
21. Riddoch J. Evaluation of practice. Physiotherapy 1991;77:439-44.
22. Keating JC, Giljum K, Menke JM, et al. Towards an experimental chiropractic: time series designs. J Manipulative Physiol Ther 1985; 8(4):229-38.
23. Rison RA. A guide to writing case reports for the Journal of Medical case reports and Biomed Central research Note. J Med Case Reports 2013;7:239.
24. Munjal YP, Prakash A, Pangtey G, editors. Pearls On Scientific Paper Writing. An Official Publication of Physicians Research Foundation. New Delhi, India; 2017.

CHAPTER

11

Ethical and Legal Issues in Research and Publication

Putul Mahanta, Mukesh Yadav

Research scholars in respect to medical education, need to possess sound knowledge and clear perspective in their relevant field and academic curriculum hardly include such experiences and skills—neither taught nor shared. Mastery and proficiency on the subject will help a medical writer in dealing with issues of research misconduct which might be challenging both in legal as well as ethical aspects in their experiments, studies, and publication. In this regard few aspects in research misconduct will be focused along with relevant ethical and legal concerns in publications.

RESEARCH ETHICS INVOLVING HUMAN PARTICIPANT[1]

Research ethics provides us the guidance for the responsibly conducting biomedical research, i.e. research involving animal and human subjects defined by principles, regulations, and laws both international and national.

Basic Objectives

- To protect the human participants (HPs).
- To ensure that the research is conducted in a way that serves the interests of individuals, groups and/or society as a whole.
- To examine specific research activities and projects for their ethical soundness looking at issues, such as the management of risk, protection of confidentiality, and the process of informed consent.
- Builds trust public accountability and public support for science.

The continued educational support on legal and ethical research might be helpful to graduates and scholars in preventing difficulties arising out of their research and publications.[2]

An outline of ethical and legal issues in research is an effort to protect human subjects engaged in biomedical research. It discusses the establishment of international, national, organizational, and institutional procedures designed to protect HPs. This chapter provides a detailed summary of the principles of ethical codes for research and their origins. It also includes discussions of the most commonly encountered ethical issues ranging from the initial decision to undertake the project, through the selection and application of the various research procedures, to the analysis and interpretation of the data.[3]

ETHICAL PRINCIPLES OF RESEARCH[4]

Biomedical research (BMR) that involving HPs raises lots of unique and complex ethical, legal, social, and political issues and is exclusively interested in the analysis of ethical issues that are raised when people are involved as participants in the research. Therefore with the HP it should be conducted in accordance with the four basic ethical principles, namely:

1. Autonomy (respect for person/participant)
2. Beneficence
3. Nonmaleficence (do no harm)
4. Justice.

The guidelines laid down are directed at application of these basic principles to research involving HPs.

WHY ETHICS IS IMPORTANT?

In law a man is guilty when he violates the rights of others. In ethics he is guilty if he only thinks of doing so. A law is an external check to a person's actions; ethics on the other hand is usually an internal guide. One would be held guilty, if he violates the laws related to the vulnerable sections of the society like children, women, elders, backwards classes, etc. But in ethical terms the person has committed the sin, the moment he thought of taking that shameful step.[5]

As per law killing a *peacock* is crime, but killing a *rat* is acceptable. *Ethics* goes beyond that *distinction* and mere *intent of killing* anyone is sufficient to prove the guilt, as *life is life* whether it is a peacock, rat or even an insect.

Ethics is needed in research and publication. If somebody violet ethics then law come in force as nobody is above the law.

Another good example of publication misconduct is plagiarism. It is a growing burning problem in *medical research* and probably the most common ethical issue *corrupting* medical writing. It threatens the *integrity of academic research* and *publication*. It handicaps the true findings. A case example is shown in Box 11.1.

Box 11.1: Plagiarism case[6]

The former Vice Canceller of Delhi University has been accused of cheating and misappropriating some genetic material from the university's science lab on a complaint filed by Saradhi, now a professor of Environmental Studies in Delhi University. Irrespective of whether the claims are true or false, it is good to know that researchers in India take plagiarism seriously. Even German professors are caught in plagiarism. It is UNIVERSAL.

BACKGROUND[7]

The shocking details of the post second world war (1939–45) trial of German medical practitioners were conducting experiments on HPs:

- Without their consent
- Exposing them to grave risk of death or permanent impairment of their faculties
- It raised grave concern about subjecting human subjects to medical research.

Thus the first International Statement on the ethics of medical research using human subjects was the Nuremberg Code that was formulated in 1947. Although informed consent for participation in research was recorded in 1900, the Nuremberg Code highlighted the essentiality of voluntariness of this consent.

Declaration of Helsinki, 1964–2008

The Declaration of Helsinki is a set of ethical principles regarding human experimentation developed for the medical community by the World Medical Association (WMA).[8] It was widely regarded as the cornerstone document of human research ethics.[9-12] It is not a legally binding instrument in international law, but instead draws its authority from the degree to which it has been codified in, or influenced, national or regional legislation and regulations.[12] Its role was described in following words: "Even though the declaration of Helsinki is the responsibility of the WMA, the document should be considered the property of all humanity"—Brazilian Forum, 2000.

Timeline (WMA Meetings) on Helsinki Declaration[13]

- 1964: Original version. 18th Meeting, Helsinki
- 1975: First revision. 29th Meeting, Tokyo
- 1983: Second revision. 35th Meeting, Venice
- 1989: Third revision. 41th Meeting, Hong Kong
- 1996: Fourth revision. 48th Meeting, Somerset West (SA)
- 2000: Fifth revision. 52th Meeting, Edinburgh
- 2002: First clarification, Washington
- 2004: Second clarification, Tokyo
- 2008: Sixth revision, 59th Meeting, Seoul
- 2013: Seventh revision, 64th Meeting, Fortaleza.

RECENT INTERNATIONAL DOCUMENTS

- The most recent documents on ethics are those of UNESCO's
- The Universal Declaration on Human Genome and Human Rights (1997)
- The International Declaration on Human Gene Data (2003)
- Universal Declaration on Bioethics and Human Rights (2005)

- The Indian Medical Council (Professional Conduct, Ethics & Etiquettes) Regulations, 2002
- Indian Medical Council Regulations (ICMR) Guidelines on Research of Human Subjects, 2006
- Professor Ranjit Roy Chaudhury Expert Committee Report, 2013
- Schedule Y of the Drugs and Cosmetics Rules, 1945
- The Drug and Cosmetic Bill, 2013.

THE INDIAN MEDICAL COUNCIL REGULATIONS[14]

This *Regulation* may be called the Indian Medical Council (Professional *conduct*, Etiquette, and Ethics) *Regulations*, 2002 (Amended Up to 8th October 2016). Few relevant regulations relating to the professional conduct, Etiquette and Ethics for registered medical practitioners in regards to research and publications are:

Chapter: 6.2 Patent and Copy Rights—A physician may patent surgical instruments, appliances, and medicine or copyright applications, methods and procedures. It shall be unethical if the benefits of such patents or copyrights are not made available in situations where the interest of large population is involved.

Chapter: 6.6 Human Rights—The physician shall not aid or abet torture nor shall he be a party to either infliction of mental or physical trauma or concealment of torture inflicted by some other person or agency in clear violation of human rights.

Chapter: 6.8 (e) Medical Research—A medical practitioner (MP) may carry out, participate, and work in research projects funded by pharmaceutical and allied healthcare industries. The MP is obliged to know the fulfillment of certain criteria's (i) to (vii) will be a necessity for undertaking any research assignment/project funded by industry for being proper and ethical.

Thus, in accepting, such a proposal a Medical Practitioner shall:

i. Ensure that the particular research proposal(s) has due permission from the competent concerned authorities.
ii. Ensure that such a research project(s) has the clearance of national/state/institutional ethics committees/bodies.
iii. Ensure that it fulfills all the legal requirements prescribed for medical research.
iv. Ensure that the source and amount of funding is publicly disclosed at the beginning itself.
v. Ensure that proper care and facilities are provided to human volunteers, if they are necessary for the research project(s).
vi. Ensure that undue animal experimentations are not done and when these are necessary they are carried out in a scientific and a humane way.
vii. Ensure that while accepting, such an assignment a medical practitioner shall have the freedom to publish the results of the research in the greater interest of the society by inserting such a clause in the MOU or any other document/agreement for any such assignment. A good research is reproducible and has minimum bias.

Regulation: 7.22 Research—Clinical drug trials or other research involving patients or volunteers as per the guidelines of ICMR can be undertaken, provided ethical considerations are borne in mind. Violation of existing ICMR guidelines in this regard shall constitute misconduct. Consent taken from the patient for trial of drug or therapy which is not as per the guidelines shall also be interpreted as misconduct.

CLINICAL DRUG TRIAL AND LEGAL ISSUES

Over the last few decades, randomized controlled trials (RCTs) have prevailed over clinical judgment, case reports, and observational studies and became the gold evidential standard in medicine. Furthermore, during the same time frame, RCTs became a crucial part of the regulatory process whereby a new therapeutic can gain access to the drug market. Today, clinical trials are large and tightly regulated enterprises that have to comply with ethical requirements while maintaining high epistemic standards, a balance that becomes increasingly difficult as the research questions become more sophisticated.[15]

In recent past in India as many as 211 people died between January and June 2012 due to serious adverse events during clinical drug trial (CDT) in India. Many demands the necessity of bringing strict regulations with rigorous monitoring to ensure that patients do not become the unfortunate victims of CDT.[16] It has also been alleged that many of the medical professional carrying CDT outside the preview of ICMR and other ethical guidelines. Even the sexual malfunction drug tried out on mentally ill-patients in Indore without proper approval of Institutional Ethics Committee (IEC) as alleged. The issues of informed consent, proper documentation of medical records, etc. were also ignored.[17]

The WHO in 2014 issued a statement strongly advocating public disclosure of all clinical trial results in India. It is said when data is not released it means that doctors, patients, and medical regulators cannot make informed decisions.[18] Hon'ble Supreme Court of India has shown its concern for protection of human rights of those who were the research participants for clinical trials and suffered either death or serious adverse events. These research participants had not given adequate compensation or no compensation at all. A Public Interest Litigation (PIL) has been filed in the Supreme Court of India in the year 2012 by a nongovernmental organization (NGO), consequently a committee has been constituted by the Ministry of Health and Family Welfare, Government of India to look into the matter of compensation.[19,20] Recently a formula to determine the quantum of compensation in the cases of clinical trial related Serious Adverse Events (SAEs) including deaths occurring during clinical trials have been evolved by a committee formed under the Drugs and Cosmetics Rules.[5,19]

Medical fraternity doing research and clinical trial will also take care of ethical aspect and not indulge in professional misconduct by violating any of the relevant provisions of the law recently enacted and those already existed.[7,19,21]

Research work and clinical trials are need of the hour, but under strict supervision and vigilance by the newly constituted bodies. NGOs are expected to keep watch on these unethical practices by all stakeholders including multinational companies. Human rights issue of these research participants will be taken care by relevant agencies including National Human Rights Commission/State Human Rights Commission (NHRC/SHRC) and various High Courts. The Supreme Court of India will come up with clear cut guidelines while disposing PIL pending before it, so that research participants will get adequate compensation for their contribution and sacrifices for greater cause of humanity.[19]

PRINCIPLES IN ETHICAL RESEARCH[22]

- *Social value*: Study should help researchers to determine how to improve people's health or well-being.
- *Scientific validity*: Research should be expected to produce useful results and increase knowledge.
- Fair subject selection.
- *Favorable risk-benefit ratio*: Any risks must be balanced by benefits to the subjects, and/or the important new knowledge the society will gain.
- *Independent review*: Groups of people who are not connected to the research are required to give it an independent review.
- *Informed consent*: Subject must be competent; researcher must give a full disclosure; subjects must understand what the researcher tells them; subject's decision to participate must be voluntary.
- Respect for enrolled subject.

ETHICAL GUIDELINES FOR BIOMEDICAL RESEARCH: ISSUES AND FEATURES[7]

Statement of ethical guidelines for BMR on HP is known as the ICMR Code and shall consist of the following:

a. Statement of General Principles on ethical considerations involving HPs in BMR.
b. Statement of Specific Principles on Research using HPs in specific areas of BMR.

Ethical Guidelines for Biomedical Research

All institutions in the country, which carry out any form of BMR involving HPs, should follow these guidelines in letter and spirit to protect safety and well-being of all individuals. It is mandatory that all proposals on BMR involving HP should be cleared by an appropriately constituted IEC.

INSTITUTIONAL ETHICS COMMITTEE[7]

Synonymous: {[Institutional Review Board (IRB), Ethics Review Board (ERB) and Research Ethics Board (REB)], Independent Ethics Committees [IEC (Ind)]}

Basic Responsibilities

- Ensure competent review of all ethical aspects of the projects proposals
- Ensure execution free of bias and influence
- Provide advice to the researchers on all aspects of the welfare and safety of the research participants.

Composition

The IECs should be multidisciplinary and multisectorial in composition. Independence and competence are the two hallmarks of an IEC. The member of persons in an ethics committee should be kept fairly small (8–12 members). The Standard Operating Procedures (SOP) of the WHO are available at www.who.int.

Composition of IEC

1. Chairperson
2. 1–2 persons basic medical science area
3. 1–2 clinicians from various institutes
4. One legal expert or retired judge
5. One social scientist or representative of nongovernmental voluntary agency
6. One philosopher/ethicist/theologian
7. One lay person from the community
8. Member Secretary.

As per revised Schedule Y of Drugs and Cosmetics Act, 1940, amended in 2005, the ethics committee approving drug trials should have in the quorum at least one representative from the following groups:[7]

1. One basic medical scientist (preferably one pharmacologist)
2. One clinician
3. One legal expert or retired judge
4. One social scientist or representative of nongovernmental organization/philosopher/ethicist/theologian or a similar person
5. One lay person from the community.

TERMS OF REFERENCE[7]

The Terms of References should include Terms of Appointment with reference to the duration of the term, the policy for removal, replacement, resignation procedure, frequency of meetings, and payment of processing fee to the IEC for review, honorarium/consultancy to the members/invited experts, etc. and these should be specified in the SOP which should be made available to each member. Every IEC should have its own written SOPs according to which the Committee should function. The SOPs should be updated periodically based on the changing requirements.

Duty of Principal Investigator

The principal investigator is the person responsible for not only undertaking the research, but also for observance of the rights, health, and welfare of the HPs recruited for the study. He should have qualification and competence in biomedical research, methodology for proper conduct of the study. He should be aware of and comply with:

- The scientific requirements of the study protocol
- The legal requirements of the study protocol
- The ethical requirements of the study protocol.

REVIEW PROCEDURES[7]

The IEC should review every research proposal on HPs before the research is initiated. It should ensure that a scientific evaluation has been completed before ethical review is taken up. The committee should evaluate the possible risks to the participants with proper justification, the expected benefits, and adequacy of documentation for ensuring privacy, confidentiality, and the justice issues.

The IEC's member secretary or secretariat shall screen the proposals for the completeness and depending on the risk involved categorize them into three types, namely, exemption from review, expedited review, and full review.

Minimal risk would be defined as one which may be anticipated as harm or discomfort not greater than that encountered in routine daily life activities of general population or during the performance of routine physical or psychological examinations or tests.

An investigator cannot decide that her/his protocol falls in the exempted category without approval from the IEC.

Exemption from Review

Proposals which present less than minimal risk fall under this category as may be seen in following situations:

- Research on educational practices, such as instructional strategies or effectiveness of or the comparison among instructional techniques, curricula, or classroom management methods.

Exceptions:

- When research on use of educational tests, survey or interview procedures, or observation of public behavior can identify the HP directly or through identifiers, and the disclosure of information outside research could subject the participant to the risk of civil or criminal or financial liability or psychosocial harm.
- When interviews involve direct approach or access to private papers.

STATEMENT OF GENERAL PRINCIPLES[7]

1. Principles of essentiality
2. Principles of voluntariness, informed consent and community agreement

3. Principles of nonexploitation
4. Principles of privacy and confidentiality
5. Principles of precaution and risk minimization
6. Principles of professional competence
7. Principles of accountability and transparency
8. Principles of the maximization of the public interest and of distributive justice
9. Principles of institutional arrangements
10. Principles of public domain
11. Principles of totality of responsibility
12. Principles of compliance.

Principles of Essentiality

After careful consideration of all aspect it should be concluded that the research proposal is:

- Necessary for the advancement of knowledge
- For the benefit of all members of the human species
- For the ecological and environmental well-being of the planet.

Principles of Voluntariness, Informed Consent and Community Agreement

While obtaining informed consent following issues should be cleared:

- When participant is incapable of giving consent
- Applicability of cardinal principles of informed consent and voluntariness
- Cardinal principles to be observed throughout the research and experiment, including its aftermath.

Where the HP is incapable of giving consent and it is considered essential that research or experimentation be conducted on such a person incompetent to give consent, the principle of voluntariness and informed consent shall continue to apply and such consent and voluntariness shall be obtained and exercised on behalf of such research participants by someone who is empowered and under a duty to act on their behalf.

Applied use, so that:

- Research participants are continually kept informed of any and all developments as far as they affect them and others
- Any community or group or individuals
- Any legal or other obligation
- Minimal restitutive obligations.

Nature and form of the consent:

- The degree of the invasiveness
- Seriousness of the invasiveness into the concerned HP's person and privacy
- Health and life generally
- The overall purpose and the importance of the research.

Ethics committee shall decide on the form of consent to be taken or its waiver based on the degree of risk that may be involved.

Principles of Nonexploitation

As a general rules research participants should be remunerated irrespective of the social and economic condition or status, or literacy or educational levels attained by the research participants kept fully apprised of all the dangers arising in and out of the research, so that they can appreciate all the physical and psychological risks as well as moral implications of the research whether to themselves or others, including those yet to be born.

Human participants should be so selected that the burdens and benefits of the research are distributed without arbitrariness, discrimination or caprice.

Each research should include an in-built mechanism for compensation for the HPs either through insurance cover or any other appropriate means.

It should cover all the foreseeable and unforeseeable risks by providing for remedial action and comprehensive after care including treatment during and after the research.

To ensure that immediate recompense and rehabilitative measures are taken in respect of all affected, as and when necessary.

Principles of Privacy and Confidentiality

Identity and records of HPs of the research are as far as possible should be kept confidential. That no details about identity of said HPs, which would result in the disclosure of their identity are revealed without valid, scientific, and legal reasons which may be essential for the purposes of therapeutics or other interventions, without the specific consent in writing of the HPs concerned, or someone authorized on their behalf after ensuring that the said HPs do not suffer from any form of hardship, discrimination or stigmatization as a consequence of having participated in the research or experiment.

Principles of Precaution and Risk Minimization

Due care and caution is taken at all stages of the research and experiment from its inception as a research idea to its subsequent research design to conduct of the research or experiment.

Requisite steps are taken to ensure that both professional and ethical reviews of the research are undertaken at appropriate stages so that further specific guidelines can be laid down, necessary directions can be given in respect to conduct of a research or experiment.

Principles of Professional Competence

Whereby the research is conducted at all times by competent and qualified persons who act with total integrity and impartiality, who have been made aware of, and who are mindful of, preferably through training, the ethical considerations are to be borne in mind in respect of such research or experiment.

Principles of Accountability and Transparency

Whereby the research should be conducted in a fair, honest, impartial, and transparent manner after full disclosure by those associated with the research of each aspect of their interest in the research.

Conflict of interest that may exist should be looked for:

Whereby, subject to:

- The principles of privacy and confidentiality
- The rights of the researcher

- Full and complete records of the research inclusive of data and notes are retained for such reasonable period as may be prescribed or considered necessary for the purposes of post-research monitoring, evaluation of the research, conducting further research (whether by the initial researcher or otherwise) and in order to make such records available for scrutiny by the appropriate legal and administrative authority, if necessary.

Principles of Maximization of the Public Interest and of Distributive Justice

Whereby the research or experiment and its subsequent applicative use are conductive and used to benefit all human kind and not just those who are socially better off but also the least advantaged; and in particular, the research participants themselves and or the community from which they are drawn.

Principles of Institutional Arrangements

Whereby there shall be a duty on all persons connected with the research:

- To ensure that all the procedures required to be complied with
- All institutional arrangements required to be made in respect of the research
- Its subsequent use or application are duly made in a bonafide and transparent manner
- To take all appropriate steps to ensure that research reports, materials, and data connected with the research are duly preserved and archived.

Principles of Public Domain

Whereby the further research, experimentation and evaluation, the emanating from such research is brought into the public domain, so that its results are generally made known through scientific and other publications (Need for publication). Subject to such rights as are available to the researcher, those associated with the research under the law in force at that time (Patent and Copyrights, Respect for IPR).

Principles of Totality of Responsibility

Whereby the professional has a moral responsibility, for due observance of all the principles, guidelines or prescriptions laid down generally or in respect of the research or experiment in question, revolves on all those:

- Directly or indirectly connected with the research or experiment including the researchers
- Those responsible for funding or contributing to the funding of the research
- The institution or institutions where the research is conducted
- The various persons, groups or undertakings who sponsor, use or derive benefit from the research, market the product (if any) or prescribe its use, so that inter alia, the effect of the research or experiment is duly monitored and constantly subject to review and remedial action at all stages of the research or experiment and its future use.

Principles of Compliance

There is a general and positive duty on all persons, conducting, associated or connected with any research entailing the use of HPs to ensure that both the letter and the spirit of these guidelines, as well as any other norms, directions, and principles which have been specifically laid down or prescribed and which are applicable for that area of research or experimentation are scrupulously observed and duly complied.

These 12 principles laid down under statement on general principles are common to all areas of biomedical research. The specific issues are mentioned under relevant topics.

STATEMENT OF SPECIFIC PRINCIPLES

- Clinical Evaluation of Drugs, Devices, Vaccines, Diagnostics, Herbal Remedies
- Epidemiological Studies
- Human Genetics and Genomic Research
- Research in Transplantation Research
- Assisted Reproductive Technologies.

REFERENCES

1. MedStar Physician Partners.Introduction to research ethics involving human subjects. [cited 2017 June 6]; Available from: URL: http://www.sitelms.org/mpp/catalog/course/details/?course id=16759&mode=enroll&name=Introduction+to+Research+Ethics+Involving+Human+Subjects
2. Regmi K. Ethical and legal issues in publication and dissemination of scholarly knowledge: A summary of the published evidence. J Acad Ethics 2011;9:71.

3. Meltzoff J. Ethics in teaching, ethics in research (online). J Aggress Malt Trauma. 2008;11(3):311-36. [cited 2017 May 27]; Available from: URL:http://dx.doi.org/10.1300/J146v11n03_03
4. Walton N. What is research ethics? In: Research Ethics.ca (online). [cited 2017 May 27]; Available from: URL:https://researchethics.ca/what-is-research-ethics/
5. Insights. [cited 2017 June 5]; Available from: URL:http://www.insightsonindia.com/2016/01/23/9-law-man-guilty-violates-rights-others-ethics-guilty-thinks-discuss-meaning-quote-suitable-examples/
6. PTI. Plagiarism case: Court grants exemption to Deepak Pental. [cited 2017 May 27]; Available from URL:http://economictimes.indiatimes.com/articleshow/46968352.cms?utm_source=contentofinterest&utm_medium=text&utm_campaign=cppst
7. ICMR. Ethical guidelines for biomedical research on human participants. 2006. [cited 2011 Dec 12]; Available from: URL:http://www.icmr.nic.in/ethical guidelines.pdf
8. World Medical Association. Declaration of Helsinki: ethical principles for medical research involving human subjects. JAMA 2013;310(20):2191-4.
9. WMA Press Release: WMA revises the Declaration of Helsinki. 9 October 2000.
10. Bošnjak S. The declaration of Helsinki: The cornerstone of research ethics. Archive of Oncology 2001;9(3):179-84.
11. Tyebkhan G. Declaration of Helsinki: the ethical cornerstone of human clinical research. Indian J Dermatol Venereol Leprol 2003;69(3):245-7.
12. Delon H, FlussSev S. The World Medical Association's Declaration of Helsinki: Historical and contemporary perspectives. 5th draft. July 24, 2001.
13. Declaration of Helsinki. Timeline (WMA meetings). [cited 2017 June 3]; Available from: URL:https://en.wikipedia.org/wiki/Declaration_of_Helsinki
14. Medical Council of India. Indian Medical Council Regulations, 2002. New Delhi, 2002 March 11 [cited 2017 May 27]; Available from: URL:http://mciindia.org/RulesandRegulations/CodeofMedicalEthicsRegulations2002.aspx

15. Nardini C.The ethics of clinical trials. Ecancermedicalscience. 2014;8:387. [cited 2017 June 2]; Available from: URL:https://www.ncbi.nlm.nih.gov/pmc/articles/PMC3894239/
16. No fewer than 211 people died. The Nation. January 30, 2012; issue [cited 2017 May 27]; Available from: URL:issuu.com/thenation/docs/january_30__2012
17. Ashish Gaur. Sexual malfunction drug tried out on mentally ill patients in Indore. The Times of India. December 20, 2011. [cited 2017 May 27]; Available from URL:http://timesofindia.indiatimes.com/city/indore/Sexual-malfunction-drug-tried-out-on-mentally-ill-patients-in-Indore/articleshow/11174168.cms
18. Nagarajan R. SC Notice to Govt on Rotavac trials data. July 08, 2016 [cited 2017 May 27];Available from URL:http://epaperbeta.timesofindia.com/Article.aspx?eid=31808&articlexml=SC-notice-to-govt-on-Rotavac-trials-data-08072016019021
19. Yadav M, Thakur PS, Rastogi P. Compensation issue in clinical trials recent Indian scenario. J Indian Acad Forensic Med 2014;36(2):160-8.
20. RM Lodha J, Anil R Dave J. Swasthya Adhikar Manch, Indore & Anr. vs. Min. of Health & Family Welf. And Ors. WP (C) 33 of 2012, Order dated: 3rd January 2013, with W.P.(C) No.79 of 2012. [cited 2017 May 31]; Available from: URL:http://courtnic.nic.in/supremecourt/temp/wc%203312p.txt
21. MCI. Minutes of the meeting of the Ethics Committee held on 20th November, 2012 at 09:00 A.M. in the Council Office, Sector - 8, Pocket- 14, Dwarka, New Delhi – 77. [cited 2017 May 31]; Available from: URL:http://www.mciindia.org/meetings/Ethics/2012/Minutes_20.11.2012.pdf
22. Research ethics: How to treat people who participate in research. [cited 2017 June 3]; Available from: URL:https://bioethics.nih.gov/education/FNIH_BioethicsBrochure_WEB.PDF

CHAPTER

12

Road Map of Submitting Manuscript for Best Acceptance

Purnima Barua, Putul Mahanta

The obvious goal of most research works is to reach out to appropriate readers. Therefore, some important points should be kept in mind before submitting to a journal for acceptance. The first question to ask yourself is, "Do I have a story to tell?" Editors and reviewers look for original and innovative research that adds to their field of study, or immediately impacts patient care. This means that your conclusions must be sound and based on sufficiently robust data. Secondly, ask yourself, "Is there an audience for my research findings?" The more original and innovative your research, the more people will be interested in it. Consider whether your research is of interest to a local, regional or international audience. Identifying your audience is a major factor in selecting the right journal to submit your manuscript to.[1,2]

There are several types of articles, viz. letters and rapid or short communications, review papers, full articles, micro-article formats, etc. If you are unsure of which type of article to write, discuss your options with your guide, colleagues, and friends. Once you have decided to write a full article, follow the guidelines of the journal you would consider sending your article to and the general guidelines for scientific writing as mentioned in the previous chapter.

Finding the right journal for your article can be a key to reaching your target audience. You should take into consideration the type of article you would like to publish. Check the references in your article, to give an indication of the possible journals of interest. Read the journal's aims and scope on the journal's homepage. Read or download the journal's guidelines for the authors. Check if the journal is invitation-only; some journals only accept articles after inviting the author to submit. Check the journal's performance for review and publication timelines. Follow the thumb rule of submitting to only one journal at a time.[1]

After going through all the previous chapters, you are now in the very best position to give a final touch of your paper for submission. For best acceptance, you can self-review your own paper to minimize the mistakes.

SELF-TECHNICAL REVIEW

In conducting your self-technical review, please consider the guidelines shown as follows:

- *Check the type of your article*: /   / Review Paper /   / Original Paper /   / Case Report /   / Critical Review /   / Book Review /   / Other.
- The "*Title*" of your paper, whether it reflects your content or not, as great title entices the audience to read on; a poorly titled article may never draw the attention of its target readers.

- *Authors sequences* as it might invite lots of issues, like conflict among authors and others, etc.
- Structured *abstract* and *keywords* whether appropriately arranged or not?

It is essential to arrange the abstract as *IMRaD* (Introduction, Methods, Results, and Discussion) format in the case of original paper, though it may differ from case presentation and thesis writing, which has already been discussed in the previous chapters.

Selecting appropriate keywords is very much important, as discussed. Keywords are used by abstracting and indexing services; choosing the right ones can increase the chances of your article being found by other researchers.

- *Body of the text*: One should keep the introduction brief, as discussed in the previous chapter. It should give context and background, but should not be a history lesson. The introduction should state the problem being investigated, its contextual background, and the reasons for conducting the research.
- *Materials and methods*: As mentioned in *Chapter 6*, this section should be detailed enough that readers can reproduce your research, and assess whether the methods justify the conclusion or not. Check whether sound method is used or not? The material and methods used in your study should be mentioned. It may include laboratory experiments, statistical calculations/computations, and comparison of existing literature, etc.
- *Results*: In this section, you will be presenting the actual results of the analysis, which you have made based on your chosen methodology. Ensure if it has been described with a very brief statement along with tables and figures, etc., as described in *Chapter 7*.

- *Discussion and conclusions*: Here the meaning of your results should be described, especially in the context of what was already known about the subject. Take care not to summarize your article—that's what the abstract is for. Ensure that this part is well-described as per the guidelines mentioned in *Chapter 8*.

  To summarize, make sure that:
  - Your results directly support your conclusions
  - You use specific expressions and quantitative descriptions
  - You only discuss what you defined early in the paper—do not introduce the reader to a whole new vocabulary. If you missed an important term, go back to the introduction and insert it
  - All interpretations and speculations should be based on fact, and not imagination.
- After conclusion, do not forget to mention about the acknowledgments, conflict of interest, ethical clearance, consent letter, author declaration part, etc. as mentioned in *Chapter 9*.
- *References* are an integral part of a paper. So do not miss or dilute this section. Remember, a good paper may be rejected on the basis of poor referencing.
- *Language quality*: Scientific article should report your findings and conclusions as clearly and concisely as possible. To achieve this:
  - Try to avoid unnecessary words or phrases—keep it simple
  - Use active writing when possible

- Tense is important. For known facts and hypotheses, use the present tense. But use the past tense when referring to experiments you have conducted. And also use the past tense to describe results
- Proofread carefully to see if you left out any words.

Your manuscript should be written in perfect scientific English before submission to the journal and your paper should be free of grammatical, spelling, and other common technical errors. Software like spellchecker may be useful for checking grammar, spelling, punctuation, etc., but remember, they do not catch all mistakes.[3] Once you have checked (and re-checked!) your manuscript, you are ready to submit it to the journal editor via the submission and peer review system.

ACCEPTANCE LETTER

You may be lucky if your paper is accepted without any changes in your article. However, the same may be rejected with a note for recorrection and resubmission as shown in Table 12.1.

Therefore, self-technical review (Table 12.2) is necessary to minimize the rejection rate and author may refer to the guidelines as mentioned in the IJHRMLP journal.[4]

PEER REVIEWER PROCESS[6,7]

The peer reviewers help to find out the soundness, significance, and originality of the paper, and can suggest improvements to the manuscript you submitted. On his/her recommendation, editor/s take/s the decision whether he/she is to accept with revisions or

Table 12.1: Format of reviewer's or editor's comments on submitted paper
• Not submitted as per instruction to author of the journal • Accepted as is or with minor editorial changes or clarifications • Provisionally accepted • Minor technical issues need attention • Minor problems exist in presentation (organization, length, logic, conclusions, etc.) • Provisionally not accepted • Significant technical issues need correction • Major problems exist in presentation • Not accepted (does not fulfill the journal criteria) • Subject matter is not suitable for publication • Technical content of article is not sound • Technical content of article lacks sufficient substance

Table 12.2: Tips for self-technical review[5]
• Is the rationale for this work well stated? • Are the objectives clearly stated? • Were sound methods used? • Are assumptions described and their reasonableness supported or rejected? • Are limitations and uncertainties in the data and analyses given? • Were alternative hypotheses and interpretations adequately considered? • Are the results presented in an objective, unbiased fashion? • Were the objectives of the study met? • Are the conclusions supported by the data? • Is the organization of the article logic? • Is the writing clear, concise, and precise?

reject a manuscript. Chances of rejection are less if you review your paper yourself. To give a good score, the peer reviewers use journal checklist as per their own guidelines which help to evaluate the scholarly content of scientific value and look for the originality. They also check the references for its correctness. The peer reviewer will look closely at your methodology and the validity of your data, and consider your ethical approach. They will then recommend changes before your manuscript is accepted for publication.

More than one million scientific articles are published each year, and that number is rising. So, it is increasingly important for you to find ways to make your article stand out.[8]

Decision-making: The process of modification by the authors, reappraisal by the original reviewers, and editors' analysis continues till the manuscript is either deemed fit for publication, or rejection. The final acceptance letter is, however, issued only after the manuscript clears the technical and language editing by one of the editors.[9] Top 10 reasons for rejection of manuscripts in Indian Pediatrics[10] journal are as shown in Table 12.3.

Peer review is a long process. Therefore, submitting to an appropriate journal and following the guidelines of that journal would save a lot of time. One should submit to one journal at a time. This would save us from embarrassment of withdrawing later. All the sections should be meticulously written and should reflect what it is meant to. References should be written with great care and only one style should be used at a time. Language should be simple and the scientific content should be obvious. One should try to minimize common errors such that the peer reviewer accepts the manuscript as such or with modification.[11]

Table 12.3: Percentage and reason of rejection of article

	Reason for rejection	*Percentage*
1.	Absence of a message	54.5
2.	Poor originality	43.5
3.	Poor methodology	28.2
4.	Not relevant to journal	25.4
5.	Overinterpretation of results	25.4
6.	Inappropriate writing style/grammar	24.2
7.	Inaccurate/inconsistent data	17.0
8.	Poor statistical analysis	9.8
9.	Insufficient data	8.0
10.	Unsatisfactory illustrations/tables	5.2

More than one reason might be operating for a given manuscript.

On rejection, the comments and suggestions should be considered in a positive light. Each submission should be a learning experience.

Though not mandatory, a cover letter is a necessity which not only says that you are submitting the paper or article to journal, but it also implies that your paper is not being considered elsewhere and you have the permission of all the co-authors, etc. The author should also write few lines about the novelty of his/her research works. The cover letter should be appropriately addressed.[11] Also suggest potential referees if asked for by the journal. By suggesting appropriate referees, you maximize the chances that your paper will get an appropriate review. One should try and avoid the obvious conflicts of interest like suggesting naming colleagues from the same institution, co-workers, etc.[11]

REFERENCES

1. Understanding the publishing process: How to publish in scholarly journals. Elsevier.com. [cited 2017 May 30]; Available from: URL:https://www.elsevier.com/_data/assets/pdf_file/0003/91173/Brochure_UPP_April2015.pdf
2. Elsevier publishing campus. [cited 2017 June 2]; Available from: URL:https://library.kku.ac.th/library2013/dmdocuments/elsevier.pdf
3. AJE. Improve the chances of having your paper accepted with academic journal experts. [cited 2017 June 2]; Available from: URL:http://www.academicjournalexperts.com/
4. Guidelines for reviewers. IJHRMLP. [cited 2017 June 4] Available from: URL:http://ijhrmlp.org/guideline.php
5. Trop J Pharm Res. [cited 2017 June 2]; Available from: URL:http://www.tjpr.org/home/reviewer_form.doc
6. Get noticed. Promoting your article for maximum impact. [cited 2017 June 2]; Available from: URL:http://www.andjrnl.org/pb/assets/raw/Health%20Advance/journals/jand/getnoticed.pdf
7. Peer review process. [cited 2017 June 2]; Available from: URL:http://submit.nursing.newnonmun.com/data/1.peer_review_process.pdf
8. Elsevier publishing campus. How to get your research article noticed. [cited 2017 June 2]; Available from: URL:https://www.publishingcampus.elsevier.com/pages/122/Colleges/College-of-Networking/Getting-noticed.html?PAGE_NR=122
9. Gupta P, Kaur G, Sharma B, et al. What is submitted and what gets accepted in Indian pediatrics: Analysis of submissions, review process, decision making, and criteria for rejection. Indian Pediatrics 2006;43(17): 478-89.

10. Gupta P, Kaur G, Sharma B, et al. What is submitted and what gets accepted in Indian Pediatrics: Analysis of submissions, review process, decision making, and criteria for rejection. Indian Pediatrics 2013; 50:77-83.
11. "What Editors want: paving the way to publication" Do's and Don'ts" when submitting papers by Pat Walsh and Tom Mommsen. [cited 2017 May 30] Available from: URL: http://www.sicb.org/students/Dos_and_Donts.pdf

Index

Note: Page numbers followed by *t* refer to table.

A

B

C

S

T

V